TEACHINGS OF THE MOUNTAIN HERMIT OF MANDONG

TAKING REFUGE AND AROUSING BODHICHITTA EXPLAINED ACCORDING TO ATISHA'S LINEAGE

BY TONY DUFF

PADMA KARPO TRANSLATION COMMITTEE

First edition, September 2004
Second edition, December 2009; revised December 2010
ISBN Paper: 978-9937-903-18-9
ISBN E-book: 978-9937-572-48-4

Garamond typeface with diacritical marks
Designed and created by Tony Duff

Produced, Printed, and Published by
Padma Karpo Translation Committee
P.O. Box 4957
Kathmandu
NEPAL

Committee members for this book: Translation and composition, Lama Tony Duff; editorial, Tom Anderson; cover design; Christopher Duff.

Web-site and e-mail contact through:
https://www.pktc.org/pktc
or search Padma Karpo Translation Committee on the web.

CONTENTS

iii

Introduction

Karma Ngedon Tengyay was a well-known meditator from Mandong—which is in Kham, Eastern Tibet—during the nineteenth century. He was a disciple of the 15th Karmapa, Khakhyab Dorje, and a practitioner primarily of the Kagyu tradition but had extensive knowledge of the views and practices of all four of the main Buddhist traditions of Tibet. In addition, he wrote extensively and his collected works were published in several volumes.

Karma Ngedon Tengyay lived most of his life in retreat in the mountains near Chogdrong District in Tibet. Thus, he became known both as Mandong Rinpoche—the precious one of Mandong—and the Hermit of Mandong.

Also living in this area were many nomads and ordinary Tibetans to whom he showed an unusual level of concern. He gave many teachings that were specifically for the benefit of these "lower classes" as he called them, the Tibetan nomads and others who were for the most part illiterate and who had a hard time gaining access to the deeper meanings of dharma.

This book contains two of his works that were written specifically with the lay-people of his area in mind. The first is about taking refuge in the Three Jewels, which is the basis of all Buddhist practice. The second is about developing compassion which is the basis for developing bodhichitta,[1] the mind that is concerned with gaining the enlightenment of a true, complete buddha for the sake of all beings. The teaching in both is based on the Stages of the Path system of teaching that was first formulated in Tibet by the great Indian master Jowo Je Atisha and passed on after that by his disciples in a tradition of teaching that became known as the Kadampa School.

As Mandong Rinpoche himself says, he wrote these two teachings specifically so that they could be easily understood—which is not the same as saying that these texts are simplistic or easy to understand! The style of his writing is colloquial, in the Kham dialect, and uses a minimum of dharma jargon (at least compared to many other texts about the same subjects). His compassion for others and his care especially for the poorer people in his district are very evident in his writings. Although he wrote for Tibetans in the nineteenth century, his compassion was obviously very strong and his words still strike a very strong chord in every reader. For this reason, his writings have become very popular these days.

He quotes former masters extensively to make his teachings easy for his audience to understand, but especially to make it easy for his audience to take them up as practice. I have seen myself how the uneducated lower classes of Tibet for whom he

---

[1] Bodhichitta literally means "enlightenment mind" and, for the sake of continuing the process of moving the words of the Buddha's dharma into English, that is how it is referred to in the rest of this book. For extensive explanations of enlightenment mind, see our book *Shantideva's Entering the Conduct of a Bodhisatva*, ISBN 978-1-7923-7440-1, authored by Tony Duff, published by Padma Karpo Translation Committee.

was writing have the particular quality that, even if they do not understand something well, if it has been said by a former master renowned within Buddhist culture, they will accept it on faith and do whatever it advises. To a modern Buddhist, the many quotations might seem odd, but they really are effective for the audience whom he was addressing. If one can approach them in a naive way, as parables almost, they can be very effective.

Many of his quotations are from the founder of the Kadampa School, Atisha, and from his principal disciples—Dromtonpa, Phuchungwa, Chen Ngawa, and Khamlungpa. These individuals lived in the period from 1000 to 1100 C.E. Note that the style of expression in these quotations is sometimes unusual and not what we would expect. It is an earlier way of speaking that reflects a very old mind of ancient India and Tibet. I have tried to translate it so that it is readable for modern minds, but it does not always fit with our current idiom and, in that case, I have just translated it literally. This style of expression requires that we pay close attention, ponder, weigh, and consider it. The teachings certainly are worthy of the effort needed.

The overall content of Mandong Rinpoche's teaching is very Tibetan. He was talking to or writing for the common people of his area in a way that he knew would be useful to them. The message of dharma is universal of course, but the packaging varies according to the minds of the listeners. The teachings here were packaged specifically for an illiterate audience who in many cases could not access the higher reaches of dharma teachings and who belonged to a culture noteworthy for its belief in gods and demons and their various realms.

You will find in here lengthy descriptions of the hells and other lower realms. These worked well for his audience; it motivated them to do something with their lives. Well-educated people from other countries in the present time often find such descriptions to be tortuous. However, we should not be too quick to just toss them aside. Educated people have the problem of thinking that they know everything or can understand everything and therefore tend to pass over things either that they have heard before or which they feel require simple-minded belief. Given that we, as educated people, have lost faith—or even worse, been taught not to engender it—perhaps we are in just as an impoverished position as Mandong Rinpoche's listeners. They have trouble understanding intellectually but have faith; we tend to understand easily but find it hard to develop a true faith.

Note that Tibetan literature tends to use very long sentences with meaning woven into the progression of thoughts within them. Sometimes these difficult sentences can be broken down when rendering them into English, but just as often have to be retained in order not to keep the meaning woven into them. Again, they demand that we slow down and pay close attention to what is being said. Hearing the teaching correctly is a precursor to being able to contemplate it properly and that is the basis for being able to cultivate it!

FURTHER STUDY

The two main topics of this book are taking refuge in the Three Jewels and arousing and developing bodhichitta, the enlightenment mind. The first topic is extensively explained in the book *Unending Auspiciousness, the Sutra of the Recollection of The Noble Three Jewels With Commentaries by Ju Mipham, Taranatha, and Tony Duff* authored by Tony Duff and published by Padma Karpo Translation Committee, ISBN 978-9937-838-61-0. The topic of arousing and developing enlightenment mind is thoroughly covered in the book *Shantideva's Entering the Conduct of a Bodhisatva with Interspersed Commentary by Padma Karpo* authored by Tony Duff and published by Padma Karpo Translation Committee. In addition to these very extensive explanations, Padma Karpo Translation Committee has published several other books on the sutras that elucidate these topics[2].

❁ ❁ ❁

May we find the faith and trust in the Three Jewels
Needed to make headway on the path to enlightenment,
Without succumbing either to blind faith
Or to the hardened rationalism of modern times.

And with that faith in heart, may we develop the larger mind,
That concerns itself for the welfare of all beings
Without forgetting that we cannot really help them
While swarming around with them in cyclic existence.

Tony Duff,
Swayambunath,
Nepal,
December 2010

---

[2] See PKTC's shop at the address shown on the publishing data page at the front of this book.

FROM THE STAGES OF THE PATH TO ENLIGHTENMENT[3]: A SMALL INSTRUCTION ON TAKING REFUGE CALLED "THE GREAT ENTRANCE TO THE EXCELLENT HOUSE OF THE CONQUEROR'S PRECIOUS TEACHING"

Namo guru ratna traya[4]

> The incomparable teacher, through his love for
>   migrators,
> Taught an ocean of dharmas in the modes profound
>   and vast.
> The only entrance for all of them is taking refuge;
> Any of them can be properly engaged but unless this
>   is relied on,
> None can be entered, therefore this is the most
>   important of all.
> I will explain briefly and just as appears in the holy
>   ones' words

---

[3] This teaching is based on the system that came from Atisha called the Stages of the Path to Enlightenment and was passed down through the Kadampa school.

[4] Homage to the guru and the Three Jewels.

> This great entrance to the excellent house of the
>   Conqueror's precious teaching,
> The communal wealth of the faithful ones, men and
>   women.
> Supreme places of refuge, please grant your blessings
>   so that
> I and others, all migrators, accomplish all desired
>   benefit and ease!

Anyone wanting to extract the essence contained in the support of freedom and endowment[5] can indeed take up the practice of only those ones of the various holy dharmas spoken by the conqueror that suit his or her particular makeup. Nonetheless, because the only entrance for all of them is to take refuge, such a person should assiduously apply himself or herself to it. This brief explanation of taking refuge comes in three parts:

1. The means for engaging in taking refuge
2. The actual taking of refuge
3. The trainings of taking refuge

1. THE MEANS FOR ENGAGING IN TAKING REFUGE

Master Shantideva[6] said,

---

[5] A support of freedom and endowment is the physical support of a human body which is special in that it additionally has eight freedoms and ten endowments that make it suitable for dharma practice.

[6] Shantideva was an Indian master well-known for his explanations
(continued ...)

> The Capable One[7] said that orientation
> Is the root of all of virtuous dharmas.
> That root always produces a full-ripened
> Effect according to its cultivation.

What he was saying there is that the root of all is orientation[8] and faith and not only that but especially that the entrance of refuge itself depends on that faith; the greater the faith, the greater the blessings received through taking refuge because of it.

Faith is of three types: admiring faith, desiring faith, and trusting faith. We speak of admiration for a great guru or that arises on seeing the deity statues in a shrine room. The faith that arises because of it is admiring faith. The faith connected with desire for happiness, the desire to accomplish virtue, the desire to abandon evil, the desire to be emancipated from samsara, the desire for enlightenment, and so on are all cases of wanting faith. The doubtless conviction that arises in relation to the words of the guru and Buddha concerning karmic cause and

---

[6] (... continued)
of enlightenment mind. He is especially famous for his text *Entering the Bodhisatva's Conduct*; see our book *Shantideva's Entering the Conduct of a Bodhisatva*, ISBN 978-1-7923-7440-1, author Tony Duff. Note that, despite the common appearance of "bodhisattva" in Western books on Buddhism, "bodhisatva" is the correct spelling. See "satva and sattva" in the glossary.

[7] For "capable one" see the glossary.

[8] "Orientation" refers to a state of mind that sees something as worthwhile and thus takes interest in and actively pursues it.

effect, the good and bad effects of virtue and evil respectively, and so on is a trusting faith.

The method for producing these three faiths was taught previously by Atisha[9]. He said that you have to think again and again about the benefits of doing virtue and not doing evil and the faults of doing evil and not doing virtue and then, following on from that, you have to think again and again about the flaws of not having taken refuge and the benefits of having taken refuge. In addition, he said that there is a difference between taking refuge as done by outsiders and insiders[10].

The Buddha said that, if you have not taken refuge, then no matter how much you produce virtue and abandon evil you are not included as an insider, a Buddhist, because of which it is not possible to obtain emancipation. And, if you have not taken refuge, then the vows of individual emancipation, the trainings of the bodhisatva vows, and the samayas of secret mantra cannot in any way be requested or observed, nor can their benefits be obtained. Also, without refuge there is no force of

---

[9] Atisha was an Indian master who was invited to Tibet in the earlier part of the eleventh century by Lha Lama Yeshe Od, who is mentioned later in this book, in order to re-establish the dharma in Tibet after it had nearly been purged into extinction in the ninth century by King Langdarma. Atisha focussed on teaching refuge and the bodhisatva path and a stream of teachings called the Kadampa tradition developed from that. The Kadampa teachings descended from Atisha form the basis for all of Mandong Rinpoche's teachings in this book.

[10] Outsiders are non-Buddhists who follow some other spiritual or belief system and insiders are those within the Buddhist fold, those who take refuge in the Buddha according to his system.

the support[11], so evil deeds are hard to purify even when laid aside, and if because of that you do then fall into the bad states, it will be extremely difficult for you to get out from them because there will be no way for you to be guided. He spoke of many flaws of not having taken refuge.

The Buddha said that, if you are able truly to take refuge, there are unfathomable benefits. Glorious Dipankara[12], and his lineage holders and followers have summed them up as follows: that one is included as an insider, a Buddhist; that it becomes the basis for all vows; that a great accumulation of merit is completed; that bad karma and the evil deeds and obscurations produced from bad afflictions are purified; that the harms brought on by negative influences, obstructors, gods, demons, spirits and so on—humans and non-humans alike—cannot touch you; that you will not be born in the bad states of the hells, pretas, animals, and so on, or in the unfree states and, even if you have such a birth due to very strong evil deeds, you will quickly come out of it; that you will in this and later lives accomplish your goals—worldly and transcendent—just as you

---

[11] Force of the support is one of a group of four forces used to remove karmic seeds of bad actions that have been accumulated on the mindstream. The force of support is the force that comes from relying on a holy object. In Buddhism, it is one or all of the Three Jewels. Thus, without refuge in the Three Jewels, you do not have one of the key components needed to clear the karmic traces of bad action from your mindstream. That being the case, it is quite likely that you will fall into the bad states in the next life because of those karmic stains. And then, once you are there, because you do not have a refuge, they themselves cannot hold out a hand to assist you.

[12] One of Atisha's names.

wanted to accomplish them and will quickly attain buddha-hood.

The bhagavat, his regent Maitreya, Guru Rinpoche[13], and others who fully understood these things explained them extensively in the great textbooks that elucidate the sutras, tantras, and treatises on them. If you can understand those, it would be good, but for people like myself, of lesser intellectual capacity, who cannot understand those things, here are some talks given by the former gurus which are easy to understand. Milarepa[14] said this and other things,

> The three of buddha, dharma, and sangha
> Are the external places of refuge.
> I myself took refuge in them and am satisfied;
> If you too were to take refuge in them, it would be
>   good.

Glorious Atisha was the crown jewel of the five hundred Indian pandits and siddhas who had mastery over all the inner oral instructions of sutra and tantra[15], but when he came to Tibet, he taught only refuge. He eventually became known as "The

---

[13] The bhagavat is the Buddha. His regent is Maitreya who he empowered as the coming buddha. Guru Rinpoche is Padmasambhava.

[14] One of the very great yogins of the Kagyu school who has become legendary as the quintessential practitioner.

[15] In Atisha's time, it was said that there were a few hundred really great masters in India, people who knew both sutra and tantra completely. Atisha was said by many to be the greatest of them all.

Refuge Pandita"[16]. When he heard of this, he said that even just his name had become beneficial to sentient beings, and was very pleased by it.

Dromtonpa[17] said,

> The humble ones of this world do not have enemies; they put all, from high to low, above them then seek their help; once someone has become an enemy, seeking help will not work. Similarly for us, if we do not want the enemy of the three realms[18], we should seek refuge in the Three Jewels right from the beginning. Out of two people, one who knows the three pitakas[19] but has no refuge and one who has no knowledge of them at all but has an uncommonly good refuge that is uncorrupted, I will choose the latter. If there is not this kind of refuge then, even if a person knows the three pitakas, he is just doing the work of a person who tells stories consisting of bad

---

[16] Pandita is an Sanskrit word meaning a learned person, siddha is a Sanskrit word meaning an accomplished person.

[17] Dromtonpa was one of the three main disciples of Atisha and is regarded as one of the most important early masters of the Kadampa tradition.

[18] The three realms' enemy is an enemy that all sentient beings have. Once one has taken a samsaric existence, one is necessarily involved with samsara, which manifests in the form of three planes or realms of existence. If you would like to be free of the enemy, samsaric existence ...

[19] The three pitakas or three baskets is a way of referring to the whole of the Buddha's teaching. They are the sections of the teaching called Abhidharma, Vinaya, and Sutra.

dharma[20]. If there is no refuge, then the receipt of
even a hundred thousand empowerments will be of
no benefit.

Khamlungpa[21] said,

> A bodhisatva who has reached the point of not
> regressing into the world is always taking refuge.

Tolungpa[22] said,

> I went before the great yogin[23] and asked whether
> there is wisdom or not at the level of buddha and
> asked him to instruct me in the two truths. He said
> that, in order to teach whether there is wisdom or
> not at the level of buddha and also the two truths, it
> is necessary beforehand to develop good methods and
> habits and therefore, it would be necessary for me to

---

[20] This phrase refers to a person who has not developed any
spiritual qualities but who goes around presenting dharma to
others. When this kind of person explains dharma to others it is
like a person who is just telling stories to others about something
that is not real dharma.

[21] Khamlungpa is another of Atisha's main disciples. He was from
Khamlung, hence his name, and was a strong practitioner who
spent a lot of time in meditation. He was especially known for his
practice of compassion.

[22] Tolungpa is another of Atisha's main disciples. He was from
Tolung, hence his name, and was a strong practitioner who spent
a lot of time in meditation.

[23] Meaning his guru, Atisha ...

take refuge first then he would give instruction after that. Therefore, I trained in nothing else but taking refuge for six months.

When I asked the guru which of the two would be more beneficial—to have one thousand men who could protect your life or to have the vows of refuge—he said, 'Son, that first kind of dharma goes nowhere! Even if one thousand men were to save the lives of the sentient beings of the world, it would just be putting off the inevitable because all of them will die. Thus, training the mind in taking refuge is what is important. As well as that reason, every one of the buddhas of the three times has become a buddha only through refuge. Although sentient being's benefit does come from the buddhas, it comes only through taking refuge. Therefore to train in taking refuge is what is important.'

Putowa said,

The spiritual friend from Yungwa, Shakya Yontan[24], said, 'I developed conviction in the Jewels, then practised. Now as just an ordinary man from Yungwa, I am very happy'. Chen Ngawa[25] also said the same kind of thing, 'Now as just an ordinary man from Lungsho, everything is completely happy and pleasant for me'. He and others, holy ones who practise dharma, even in this life have a happiness equal to the gods. Therefore, each of us also should

---

[24] One of the great teachers of the earlier Kadampa tradition.

[25] One of the three main disciples of Dromtonpa, who was another of the very important figures of the early Kadampa.

surrender ourselves to the Jewels and then, if we practise dharma as it should be practised, in this life we too will definitely have happiness and find everything pleasant.

The yogin Trichog said,

You can say that you have received the vows of individual emancipation through those of the bodhisatva and of secret mantra but, if you have not genuinely taken refuge in your mind, then those vows are not part of the Buddha's teaching. If not, then besides not having the three sets of vows, the accumulations cannot be collected, the obscurations cannot be removed, the fruition of the three kayas cannot be obtained, and the dharma path leading to them cannot be travelled. If you do have this common basis of taking refuge, then in this life prior to death, things will turn out well and following that, the omens at death will turn out well. If you personally do not have this specific thing of taking refuge, you could explain the three pitakas but it would only produce the views of the Tirthikas[26].

---

[26] Tirthikas is the general name that the Buddha and his followers have used for non-buddhists who do practise some spiritual system. *The Illuminator Tibetan-English Dictionary* gives a clear explanation of the meaning of the term; essentially, it is a kindly spoken term that says that these are people who have started on the road to enlightenment, even if they have not yet entered the main path to enlightenment shown by the Buddha.

Neu Zur[27] said,

> For all humans, if at the time of death their faculties
> are a little clear and they have taken refuge, then,
> since the mind at death has some power, they will not
> fall into the bad states. The Three Jewels will look
> after them.

The Unequalled Dvagpo[28] said,

> What is this taking of refuge that is preliminary to
> everything? Taking of refuge is the essence of vows.
> When the mindstream has the three vows[29], the vows
> are there for all; nonetheless, for those who have not
> taken refuge, they are not.

---

[27] Neu Zur is another of the early and well-known Kadampa masters.

[28] The Unequalled Dvagpo is the common way in Tibet of referring to Gampopa. Although Gampopa later became one of the most important lineage holders of the Kagyu, he was, until his twenties, deeply involved in Kadampa practice, and was considered to be a very accomplished Kadampa practitioner. Later, after staying with Milarepa, he became Milarepa's main successor, and was then known as someone who united the sutra teaching of the Kadampas and the Mahamudra teaching of the Kagyus. Since then, this union of the two streams of teaching has always been part of the Kagyu tradition and now it is being faithfully passed on by the Mandong Hermit, himself a Kagyu practitioner.

[29] The three vows are the vows of the lesser, great, and vajra vehicles. None of them can happen unless a person has the vows of refuge first.

The meaning is that, if you were to lose refuge, it would be as though the vows become totally erased. There are causes both of refuge becoming weakened and of its being lost. Sang Phupa and other yogins[30] have said the same.

Chen Ngawa said,

> Having been blessed by those holy ones[31], I developed the ability in general to stay in many different samadhis each for many days at a time and specifically developed excellent samadhis of the development and completion stages[32]. Now though, I have put all that aside and only take refuge.

> These words have been given out of affection for a few of you who have sincere interest. I have given you what are called the oral instructions for death[33] but these instructions for death have nothing in them that is greater than the taking of refuge. If you die while taking refuge with a heart and mind that has conviction in the Three Jewels, it will send you ahead

---

[30] Sang Phupa was yet another early Kadampa practitioner and other yogins refers to others like him, who knew the Buddha's dharma and practised it accordingly.

[31] Meaning that he has received the instructions of his Kadampa teachers and thus has their blessings.

[32] The samadhis or concentrations of the development and completion states are the concentrations of the two main parts of the vajra vehicle as a whole.

[33] The instructions on how to prepare for death in this life and how to actually die are some of the important instructions within the Kadampa tradition.

of one hundred others. If it were to drag you back behind one hundred others, even then you would not go to the bad states.

Conqueror's son[34] Khamlungpa said, "The constant taking of refuge establishes you in great accomplishment." One of his students said to him, "It seems as though I must do some propitiatory rites[35] this year because of great physical problems that can come." He replied, "If you are constantly taking refuge then how can the would-be harms of humans and non-humans affect you?"

Sharawa[36] said,

> If you familiarize your mind now with having conviction in the Three Jewels and taking refuge in them, it will guide you at the time of death and in the bardo[37], too, and you will not be born in the bad states[38]. In case you are born in the bad states, even

---

[34] "Conqueror's son" is another name for "bodhisatva".

[35] The ordinary Tibetan views sickness as the result of being attacked by spirits. There are many different rites for propitiating them to keep them happy and, as a result, for the disease to dissipate.

[36] Geshe Potowa was, together with Dromtonpa, one of the main disciples of Atisha, and Sharawa was Potowa's main successor.

[37] The bardo is the "intermediate" state between one life and the next.

[38] The bad states are the hell, preta, and animal realms which
(continued ...)

then you will be guided by taking refuge and will be emancipated.

About this Jowo Je[39] said,

> In India, a Tirthika who had accomplished the wind lasso[40] used it and brought everyone under his control except for one child. Even though he sent the wind lasso, he could not affect the child with it at all. Thinking to himself, "Has my wind lasso ability become impaired?", he tried it out on a dog and the dog died. So, thinking to himself, "I wonder what special quality this child has?", he asked the child about it and the child replied, "I have no special quality. I am always taking refuge in the Jewels". Because of this, the Tirthika also became an insider and while taking refuge went begging in populated places where there were compassionate people.
>
> He came to one particular town whose whole population had just died because of a ghost who was spreading sickness. He was unable to bear that, so, out of his compassion, he went looking for a guru who could revive them from their deathbeds. He met three yogins and said, "If you three have great

---

[38] (... continued)
collectively are the really miserable possibilities of birth within cyclic existence.

[39] Jowo Je is yet another name for Atisha.

[40] "Wind lasso" is the name of a yogic practice that leads to accomplishment of the ability to take hold of others and bend their minds to one's own wishes.

qualities, then please bring all the people from this town back from the dead. You will get whatever goods and wealth you want from doing it". The three yogins said that they would come. They went there and, in order to subdue the malevolent ghost causing the sickness, did a torma exorcism[41]. After dark, the malevolent ghost appeared in a body full of eyes, sent a wind through the window opening to blow out the oil lamp, went inside, and killed the three yogins.

Again the man went looking up and down for a guru. He met a Buddhist monk. Again, he asked for help. The monk said, "I have no qualities. We can go there for food." The monk went there and stayed there performing the taking of refuge. The man said, "Now do you have some way to appease this ghost or not? Yesterday, the malevolent ghost even killed the three yogins; I am still here because I hid myself." The bhikshu replied, "No more special appeasement than refuge is needed. You do not need to hide yourself so that you will not be seen. This is the compassionate activity that comes from performing refuge." Again that night the ghost came back and sent a draught through the window but this time was not able to blow out the oil lamp. The monk subdued the ghost. In this story of bringing back the dead, the man was Dromtonpa, and the Buddhist monk was Atisha.

---

[41] A torma exorcism involves making offerings to the beings to be exorcised and asking them to leave. The offerings are represented by a piece of dough made into a specific shape which is, in Tibetan, called a torma.

Besides this, there is the story of the Indian king called Increasing Merit who did not do any of the things that kings usually do—making royal decrees of law, fighting with the four types of armed forces, and so on—but stayed within taking refuge. Notably, the king and his subjects flourished without the appearance of any opposition. These and other stories like them appear in the Kadampa tradition's collection of dharma called *The Son's Dharma*, which consists of over twenty volumes that mostly talk only about the benefits of taking refuge.

The Conqueror's Son Thogmey[42] said,

> If you are able to give yourself over to the Three
> Jewels, blessings and ability will immediately accrue.

Dzogchen Patrul[43] said,

> It is said that if you have not taken refuge in the
> Jewels, no matter what practice of profound dharma
> you do, it does not get to the fullness of being an
> insider, a Buddhist; this is what is called, 'the
> difference between outsiders and insiders of refuge'.
> The Tirthikas also have not creating non-virtuous
> karma and attainment of the common attainments

---

[42] Thogmey Zangpo is a very famous Tibetan master of the Sakya tradition who wrote a text called *The Thirty-Seven Practices of All Buddha's Sons* about the bodhisatva's way which quickly became and still is very famous.

[43] Dza Patrul was one of the early lineage holders of the Longchen Nyingthig system of Great Completion teachings. He spent much of his life at Dzogchen Monastery in East Tibet, hence his name. He is well known for his humbleness and ability to teach dharma to all levels of people.

through meditation on deities, on channels and
winds, and so on, but, because they do not take
refuge in the Jewels, they are separated from the path
of emancipation and definitely are not emancipated
from cyclic existence.

When Siddha Thangthong Gyalpo[44] was small, he was sent by
his parents to a teacher to learn letters. After he had learned to
read, his teacher taught him the great meaning of taking refuge
and because of that, he then stayed indoors, taking refuge day
and night, in the four sessions. Later on, his unfathomable
activities for the welfare of beings were done through both
taking refuge and reciting the mani[45]. He said himself, "If the
compassionate activity, blessings, and abilities of the Jewels
were turned into form, they would not fit into the whole of
space."

The holy ones have said these and many other such things but,
concerned that this could go on too long, I will not write more.
I have gathered and arranged these small excerpts so that others
of small intelligence, like myself, could easily understand this
subject. The meaning contained in them should be thought

---

[44] Thangthong Gyalpo is another legendary figure for Tibetans.
He was known for his knowledge of sutra according to the Kadampa tradition and his practice of the Vajra Vehicle according to
Nyingma tradition. He was also very famous for having built
many bridges of iron—an essentially impossible thing to do at his
time in Tibet—across otherwise un-crossable rivers.

[45] The mani is the mantra of Avalokiteshvara. The common folk
of Tibet, even if they did not know anything else about the Buddha's dharma, did know this mantra and would recite it.

about again and again as follows. "From today until I reach enlightenment, whether good qualities in a greater or lesser amount are produced, whether happiness or sadness, goodness or badness arises, if I am not able to request refuge of the guru and Jewels, I am just another, coarse human being, aren't I?"

As far as taking refuge goes, for those who cannot recite yet or who are preparing to learn to do so or who are in the middle of learning to read and pronounce letters, their current studies are what they must work at for now. For all others, first there are those who are not able to supplicate for refuge in the guru and Jewels; for them, even though it might seem as though they are happy at the moment and that their qualities are becoming greater and greater, still, until they have obtained the levels of the noble ones they need to turn their minds away from conviction in composite phenomena[46]. For those who can supplicate for refuge in the guru and Jewels, even though it might seem that they are wretched and poor at the moment, because of taking refuge now, they will steadily become stronger in the next or later lives. Then, at some point, they will take up the path of emancipation of the higher realms. It will at that point be necessary for them to think about this again and again in order to produce as much as possible, without doubts, and from the depths of their hearts, an unchangeable resolve to exert themselves at taking refuge.

---

[46] For noble ones, see the glossary. The noble ones are those who have become spiritually advanced to the point that they have passed beyond cyclic existence. Until their levels are reached, it is essential to turn the mind away from its insistent thinking that composite phenomena are real, reliable, and so on; the Buddha said many things about this.

Putowa said,

> If you think about this over and again, trust will
> increase and then your mind will give itself over to
> the lords and, having done so, their blessings will
> come. Having found certainty in this, take refuge
> from the core of your heart and train in its trainings.
> Then whatever you do will be given over to the
> activity of the Buddha's dharma.[47]

2. The Explanation of Actually Taking Refuge

The teachings of the nine vehicles[48] distinguish various ways of
taking refuge and as a result explain many ways of doing so,
such as the outer, inner, and secret ways of taking refuge and
the four extra-secret ways of taking refuge. However, if I explain this in a general way that is common to all of these different levels of taking refuge, there are the following three topics
to consider.

1. The object of refuge

All of us have sunk into the ocean of unsatisfactoriness of cyclic
existence and because of that live in the wretchedness of various
sufferings. No other person—not our father, mother, children,
relatives, friends, gods, nagas, locale owners, etcetera—can

---

[47] The three lords of refuge are the Three Jewels.

[48] The nine vehicles are a way of presenting the entirety of the
Buddha's teaching in nine, progressive steps. The system was
introduced into Tibet from India by Padmasambhava.

protect us from this and we also cannot repel it, therefore we do need a refuge.[49]

The only being who has the ability to protect us fully is the Buddha; therefore the Buddha is suitable as an object of refuge. There are four reasons for the Buddha being suitable as an object of refuge. 1) He is liberated from his own fears; if he were not, this would be like one person drowning in water not having the ability to save another who also is drowning. 2) He is skilled in the means for taming those to be tamed; if he were not, then even if he did want to provide protection, he would not be able to fulfill the other being's need for protection in its entirety. 3) He has great compassion; if he did not, he would not necessarily give protection even if he knew how to give it. 4) He is pleased not by offerings of this and that but by development of faith, respect, and so on; if he were otherwise, he would make distinctions between the high and low, strong and weak. Therefore, he is suitable as an object of refuge for these reasons: he is liberated from his own fears; he is skilled in the methods for protecting others; he has no pause in his compassion; and he works for all without the biases of high and low, male and female, poor and rich, and so on, in other words without distinctions into close and distant. Those qualities are

---

[49] Nagas are one type of being belonging to the animal realm who usually have a lot of power and who are usually not visible to humans. They have a snake-like appearance. Locale owners are spirits from the preta realm or gods of the desire realm who have taken up residence in some locale within the human realm. As far as they are concerned, the place they live in is their territory. Humans can fall afoul of them by not appreciating that they regard themselves as the owners of that territory.

complete only in a buddha, not in anyone else. Therefore, the Buddha is called the "actual refuge".[50]

Moreover, he is the teacher, therefore he is called "the teacher". What has been taught by him is to be practised, therefore the dharma he has taught is called "the path". The way to follow that path is shown by the noble ones, therefore the sangha, or community, of noble ones is known as "the assistant". In Secret Mantra, or tantra, an additional three refuges called the three roots are taught: the root of blessings is the guru; the root of attainment is the yidam; and the root of activity is the dakinis and dharmapalas. I relation to the Three Jewels, the three roots are like this: the guru is the embodiment of all the Jewels; the yidam is the Buddha; and the dakinis and dharmapalas are an arm of the noble sangha. In that way, all three roots are contained within the Three Jewels. Therefore it is said,

> The three of buddha, dharma, and sangha
> Are the refuge for those wanting emancipation.

2. The thoughts involved with refuge

Generally, it is said that refuge becomes a completely pure refuge when the following four features have been developed. First, the qualities of the Three Jewels are understood. Second, buddha, dharma, and sangha are understood to be superior respectively to the outsider's teachers, outsider's wrong dharma, and the outsider's Tirthika supporters, and so on. Third, having understood that, a declaration of taking refuge that comes from the heart is made. Fourth is that then, even if it

---

[50] "Without distinctions into close and distant" means that he does not fall into the biasses of holding some with affection and some with aversion.

comes to one's life, refuge is never sought in anything other than the Three Jewels.

In relation to that, there are two extremely important points. Oneself and others, all sentient beings, are in a wretched state due to the various sufferings of cyclic existence, especially those of the bad migrations. Therefore, one point is to develop an unfeigned fear of this wretched state in which all of us live and to arouse as much compassion as possible for the beings in it. A second point is to have a firm trusting type of faith that thinks, "I know that the Three Jewels have the ability to protect from the unsatisfactoriness of cyclic existentence and am certain of that", and through that to surrender oneself, without any doubts, to the Three Jewels.

The reasons for the above four are explained through four faults: if there were no fear, even though you took refuge, it would just be refuge in words only; if there were no compassion for sentient beings, your refuge would become the refuge of the Lesser Vehicle; if you did not understand that the Three Jewels do have the ability to protect, strong faith in them would not arise in you; and if you did not have sufficient trust that you could truly surrender to the Three Jewels, the blessings of their compassionate activity would not enter.

3. The ritual of refuge; the refuge recital and meditation

Many different verses appear in the sutras and tantras, word and treasures, and new and old translations[51] that can be recited in

---

[51] There were two periods of the flourishing of dharma in Tibet, older and newer, and each had a period of intense translation activity that went with it. The older translations go with the

(continued ...)

order to take refuge and you can recite which of them you know and feel inspired to recite.[52]

One refuge liturgy called "The Mothers Like Space Refuge"[53] has unmatched blessings and benefit for beings. The following has been said about it: "Avalokiteshvara actually spoke it and the accomplished Thangtong Gyalpo received it, therefore recitation of it will greatly benefit unfathomable numbers of sentient beings!" This is the prayer:

> I and every one of the motherly sentient beings equal
>   to space take refuge in the guru, the precious
>   buddha;
> Take refuge in the buddha, the dharma, and the
>   sangha;
> Take refuge in the guru, yidam, and assembly of
>   dakinis;
> And take refuge in one's own mind, empty-
>   luminosity, the dharmakaya.

The way of meditating on the object of refuge is as follows. This is given according to the system of Mahamudra, and the

---

[51] (... continued)
Nyingma tradition and the newer translations go with the Kagyu, Sakya, and Gelug traditions.

[52] Word and treasures are the two main streams of Buddhist dharma that come down through the Nyingma tradition of Tibetan Buddhism.

[53] This is a refuge that Thangthong Gyalpo received in a direct vision of Avalokiteshvara and is therefore regarded as particularly effective.

like, where meditation is done on a refuge object consisting of five groups of the places of refuge. It can also be done with guru Avalokiteshvara[54] surrounded by an ocean of refuge objects or in a more condensed way as follows. Appearing in the space before you on a lotus-moon seat is the object of refuge, in essence the root guru and in appearance Avalokiteshvara the tamer of beings, white, four armed, and adorned at his crown with the lord of his family Amitabha. Brilliant light blazes out from the marks and signs[55] of his body reaching myself and others, the migrators pervading space. Thinking of us with great love, he is seated there smiling. He is surrounded by an ocean of refuge objects or they are invited and dissolve into him. Be certain that, without needing anything further, he is from the beginning the embodiment of every place of refuge. His mind is alpha purity[56], free from all elaboration, the summation of all buddhas. His speech is unceasing, various dharma doors, the summation of the holy dharma. His body with the marks and signs[57] perfectly complete is the summation of the sangha. Thus he is the summation of the Three Jewels. His mind is inseparable from that of all of the Indian and Tibetan learned and accomplished vidyadharas, and, dwelling in this great sameness of taste, he is the summation of all gurus. His channels, winds, and drops purified in place, he is the

---

[54] "Guru Avalokiteshvara" means one's guru seen as being inseparable from Avalokiteshvara, the embodiment of compassion.

[55] The marks and signs are the thirty-two major and eighty minor signs of a buddha.

[56] For alpha purity, see the glossary.

[57] The marks and signs are the thirty-two major and eighty minor signs of a buddha.

summation of the viras, dakinis, treasure masters, and wisdom dharma protectors. Thus he is the summation of the three roots. All of those are the self-knowing, primal wisdom's door of appearance, stoppageless liveliness's lustre, non-dual, unified spontaneous presence[58]—and one is certain of that through intellectual understanding, experience, or realization, whichever level one is capable of. Those of lesser abilities might not understand this but that does not matter; it is enough that they resolve that this guru Avalokiteshvara himself is the summation of all places of refuge.[59]

Before him are myself and others, all sentient beings, and in order to emancipate all of us from the problems of cyclic existence and the bad destinies and to achieve buddhahood, think the following with faith, respect, and one-pointedness: "From this time until enlightenment, regardless of whether we are happy, sad, good, bad, up or down, look on us!", then say the verses of taking refuge three, seven, twenty-one, one hundred thousand, etcetera, times according to how much freedom you have. At the end, the object of refuge melts in light and sinks into you and the blessings of compassion enter you. Think that your mind becomes dharma and that there are no

---

[58] This uses the words of profound, extra-secret Great Completion (Dzogchen). It is not possible to explain here.

[59] This explanation of taking refuge is given according to the Nyingma teachings of Great Completion. As he says, if you understand it, then you understand, and if not, it will be sufficient to do it in the simpler way that he then describes. All in all, he is teaching this refuge in a very simple way and using the deity—Avalokiteshvara—that will work for the average Tibetan who is in the audience before him.

hindrances, and then remain in equipoise. Then do this dedication:

> What all the conquerors who go in the three times
> Dedicate to, what they praise as excellent, likewise
> I also will, for the sake of the excellent conduct,
> Utterly dedicate all of my roots of merit to that.

You should constantly exert yourself at taking refuge like that. At night when you are going to sleep and in the morning on waking, train at remembering to take refuge. At times of fear such as sickness and famine, warfare and strife, enemies, robbers, bandits, thieves, serious illness, harm from negative forces and obstructors, punishment of rulers, and so on, no matter what arises, taking refuge alone is sufficient for all of it. Even if you search the third order universe[60], it will be hard to find a better ritual than taking refuge. When people like ourselves of small mind meet harmful, inimical, or obstructing beings or when there is illness, adverse circumstances, and so on and we have run out of options, the non-deceptive precious Jewels have blessings and capabilities which are inconceivable and no matter who supplicates them—male or female, beggar or rich man, strong or weak—they make no distinctions, they think of the person like a mother thinking of her child. To toss this aside in favour of reliance on worldly gods, ghosts, or men such as Brahma, Ishvara, Vishnu, or other gods, or nagas, locale owners, and so on is the height of foolishness, just like waving money in

---

[60] Third order universe is a universe containing one thousand to the power three individual world systems of the Mt. Meru type. This would be roughly equivalent to what the Western world thinks of as our universe. However, the Buddha said that there are infinite numbers of third order universes.

front of beggars. Realize that, at the time of death, if you die while actively taking refuge, it will not be possible for you to go to the bad destinies and you will have the boon of going to the good ones.

Surrendering yourself without hesitation to the fullness of this is an extremely profound point concerning the entrance of blessings. As Guru Padma[61] said,

> If you do not have confidence through faith, then the blessings of the Three Jewels are far away.

Dromton Rinpoche—and other Kadampa forefathers similarly—said,

> The refuge vows are produced while neither taking the Buddha's words as the mere words of a diviner nor taking the Buddha's blessing as the mere degree of benefit produced by a person who gets rid of ghosts. If a diviner says to you, "This year, you have bad stars to be concerned about, therefore, do this and do not do this ...", you will exert yourself at such because otherwise the thought that you have not done just as the diviner said will create great worries of impending unhappiness. The Buddha said, "Be greatly concerned about cyclic existence and the bad destinies and because of it do virtue like this and do not do evil like this". If you are convinced of what he said and do take up the practices but nothing seems to be accomplished, then please do not worry at all; this kind of talk coming from a person embodying the dharma is not like the ordinary way

---

[61] Padmasambhava.

of speaking which says, "You cannot do that just now so do this instead". The Buddha's words are very special. What he said has the meaning, "Go straight ahead on the basis of what you want and what you understand", and if you think about that, it is very, very true. No matter what the circumstances are— happy or sad, good or bad—if you can take refuge without hesitation or doubt, there is nothing, except for the full-ripening of karma[62], that the Jewels cannot protect against.

Once you have taken refuge, there are two aspects to how protection is provided. The first is the capability of the blessings of the Three Jewels; it is like a hook that they have which nothing can block. The second is your trusting faith through which you surrender yourself to them without doubts; it is like a ring. When you do not have the ring, there can be no emancipation from the unsatisfactoriness of cyclic existence. The hook is available, but without the ring there can be no effect, just like there might be a sharp hook but it will not be able to get a grip on a smooth pebble[63].

---

[62] Full-ripening of karma is one of the many ways that karma can ripen according to the teachings of Buddha. Essentially, there are some kinds of karma whose ripening is very hard to avoid; full-ripening is one of them. Taking refuge is not sufficient to prevent that kind of karmic effect; other practices have to be done on top of it to eliminate the effect.

[63] This is a standard analogy. The help that can be provided by the Three Jewels and Three Roots, too, is like a hook which can be used to grab others and bring them under protection. However,

(continued ...)

When you do understand that all that arises—whether it is happiness or sadness, goodness or badness—is the blessing of the Jewels, then faith and respect can be increased within, and your refuge will become genuine. In relation to this, there are many who do think that the arrival of happy circumstances is the compassionate activity of the Jewels. However, if they do not understand that the arrival of bad circumstances also is the blessing of the Jewels, there is a great danger that they will think, "Just by supplicating for refuge this bad thing has happened; taking refuge was useless!", and then develop wrong views because of it. Therefore, even when bad circumstances arise, you should make yourself understand, "For beginningless lives I have done various evil deeds because of which I will have to experience the almost unbearable sufferings of the bad migrations. The compassionate activity that comes from taking refuge in the Jewels has come forth as some kind of suffering for me just now so that later on the good path could be found." Being thankful to each of them and once again assiduously taking refuge is an extremely important and major point. This key point appears in the following story of the girl Excellent told by Atisha.

> There was an Indian king whose daughter was called Excellent. She had great faith in and always made offerings to and took refuge in the Jewels because of which she was venerated and praised by all. Her two wicked maid attendants were thinking, 'We three are very much the same—we are human and we are female—but she gets the greatest praise of all whereas we do not; we will bring her down!'

---

[63] (... continued)
there has to be a ring of faith and trust on our side for the protection which is on offer to be able to catch hold of us.

The three of them went to bathe in water[64]. The two said 'Bring your golden basin! We two will bring our copper basins'. When the water had filled the bathing area, the three talked about putting their basins on top of the water. The daughter said, 'I won't put it there because if I do and it gets lost, my father will scold me'. The others told her that she did not understand. If the basin really was precious gold, how could it sink into the water? Copper is precious too, so it also could not sink! Having said that, they put their copper bowls onto the surface of the water and they floated perfectly on top. The daughter, thinking, 'Is this really true?', put the golden bowl down on the water but, because gold is very heavy, it sank. The maids exclaimed, 'You have little merit! The copper bowls did not sink but the gold one did! No-one else's precious things are like this! You have gotten all of us into trouble!'

The daughter, unhappy over these words, said, 'Servants, go before the king. Tell him that the golden bowl has been lost in the water and ask him whether we can try to retrieve it again or not?' The maids went before the king and said, 'Your daughter has lost the golden basin in the water. Should we tell her to leave and go to another country?' The king said, 'Girls, do not be so small minded! What valuables do I need? Now, go and make offerings to the Jewels.'

---

[64] In ancient India, there were communal bathing places that the populace went to for bathing purposes.

The maids went off. They were in the process of bringing back horses and a small amount of food when they met a Tirthika on the road. One said to him, "This king has faith in the Buddhists. We have faith in the Tirthikas. We are going to take the girl Excellent to another country. Say that all three of us jumped into the water and killed ourselves". Having given these twisted instructions to him, the two went on their way, to the king's daughter.

One said to the daughter, "Your father the king said, 'This kind of valuable does not come even to the naga kings. Since you have not produced a son, the kingdom's power will be wasted because of you. Take this horse and get out; go to a place where I don't hear of you!'" The daughter composed a verse in reply,

> Wealth you are a mistake, your name
>   matches the meaning[65]—
> You crossed over to the opposition's side.
> Before, my faith was in the Jewels;
> Now, my faith is in the Jewels.

Then she mounted the horse.

The maids said, 'We are older than you so we will ride in front and you can ride behind'. They rode

---

[65] This is a play on words in Tibetan; the word for wealth is the same as the word for a mistake. Her wealth of the golden bowl was a mistaken thing; it turned from being helpful to her to being helpful to her enemy.

off. After a difficult ride, all three finally arrived in a new country.[66]

The king asked one of his queens what had happened and she told him that a Tirthika who arrived had said they had leapt to their death into the water. The king was deeply worried. He made vast waves of virtue by making very large offerings to the Jewels, and so on. The three had gone to a kingdom where they were unknown but, because of the power of the Jewels' blessings, they met with the queen of that country's king. After they told a little of their story, the queen realized that Excellent was a princess and took her in with the other queens of the king.

At that time, Noble Avalokiteshvara was thinking of making a human manifestation for the sake of migrators. Looking about for the right parents, he saw the girl Excellent. Thinking that her great faith in the Jewels would make her a good mother for the manifestation, the manifestation entered her womb. When the child was about to be born, one of the nursemaids said to the king, 'Are you ready to go and greet the new mother?' The king was slow in coming and the child was born before he arrived. The maid gave drugged liquor to Excellent who then lost consciousness. The the corpse of a puppy was put in place of the newborn son and the son was hidden behind a stairway. The king, on asking after the child, was told that the corpse of a dog could not be shown to him. Therefore the king did not get to see

---

[66] In India, persons of higher rank go at the front and those of lesser rank go behind them. Thus the servants were putting themselves at a higher rank and puting the daughter below them.

the child. The king was not pleased and Excellent,
the nursemaid, and the two wicked women were to
be punished.

The manifested son showed a miracle from his place
below the stairs and the two maids were shifted to
and hidden in various places; finally they were hidden
in a garden and a tree of precious substances grew. A
sheep nibbled at the tree and because of it gave birth
to a lamb of precious substances. When the shepherd
thought, 'Now what should I do?' the lamb replied,
'Please leave me right here!' The shepherd looked
about and found a wondrous, emanated palace and
met the emanation of Avalokiteshvara inside. The
king heard about this and asked about it. When he
heard the story, he was filled with regret. He told the
queen to go before the son and lay aside[67] her faults.
Then he said to Excellent, "Queen Excellent, you can
be happy now. This emanation son, through various
miracles, will do great works for migrators".

In that story, even though the maras[68] connected with the
wicked maids made various efforts to overcome the girl Excellent, because she had taken refuge with an unperverted faith,
she was able to fulfil her human life completely. With this in
mind, Kongtrul Rinpoche[69] said,

---

[67] For lay aside, see the glossary.

[68] For maras see the glossary. In this context it means "negative
forces".

[69] This refers to the first Jamgon Kongtrul, a very great master of

(continued ...)

It is not enough just to recite just the words of refuge. It is necessary to have conviction about the Jewels from the depths of your mind. If you do, there is nothing from which the compassionate activity of the Jewels cannot protect you. If you have some very bad karma that has to ripen in this life, the compassionate activity of the Jewels will appear as the unfortunate result of that karma, though if you have faith, they will definitely protect you in subsequent lives. When smaller undesired events occur, if you say that it is not the compassionate activity of the Three Jewels or if you place your hopes in divinations, special rituals, medical examinations, and so on, this is just a sign of a small mind. In any given situation, the compassionate activity of the Jewels might not appear but that is your fault for not supplicating them; it is not possible for the Jewels themselves to be without blessings.

If you do not know these kinds of key points, even though you push yourself to take refuge, it will not be authentic. Sangyay Pon said,

> Our taking of refuge, like the female practitioner who entered the temple and said, "I take refuge in Arya Palo", is like a con-man trying to sell something. In it there is no refuge, only words.[70]

---

[69] (... continued)
East Tibet in the nineteenth century.

[70] This is a story in the Buddhist tradition about a woman who went to Arya Palo to seduce him. She started out with the nice

(continued ...)

In other words, the key points of how to take refuge also have to be known.

3. THE TRAININGS OF TAKING REFUGE

This has two parts:

1. Training in the vows of refuge
2. Trainings that are like precepts of refuge

1. Training in the Vows of Refuge

This has eleven parts: three advices concerning what to stop doing, three concerning what to start doing, and five common ones.

The three to stop doing are as follows:

1. Having taken refuge in the Buddha, it is not all right to take refuge in worldly deities such as Brahma, Ishvara, and Vishnu[71] or beings such as gods, nagas, locale owners, and so on. If you perform Sang rituals[72], erect prayer flags, and so on for the

---

[70] (... continued)
words of seeking his assistance which was a standard ploy in Indian culture when a woman was trying to seduce a man.

[71] These are the three great gods in which main Indian religion other than Buddhism, the Hindu religion, places its faith.

[72] "Sang" is a ritual that was introduced into Tibet by Padmasambhava for clearing negativity. Tibetans commonly did Sang and other practices in which they invoked various gods and demons and asked for protection. He is saying that this is all right but that one must not regard such beings as being any more than a
(continued ...)

purpose of holding harmful acts done by such beings as the ones just mentioned at bay, then understand that the powerful beings invoked in these ceremonies are just temporary assistants being used for the sake of accomplishing the activities of enlightenment.

2. Having taken refuge in the dharma, it is not all right to harm sentient beings. The harm that could be done to sentient beings—killing, piercing the noses of animals, castrating animals, overloading beasts of burden, beating and hitting, and so on—should be abandoned to the best of your ability.

3. Having taken refuge in the sangha, it is not all right to associate with Tirthikas. There are no real Tirthikas in Tibet[73] but people who are their equivalent—wrongdoers, and especially those who have no faith in and who would harm the Jewels or nay say them—should not be taken up as comrades. Such types of bad company should be abandoned.

The three to start doing are as follows:

1. Physical representations, pictures, and so on of the Buddha should not be put down just anywhere. Atisha at one time was once asked whether a painted image of the Buddha was good or not. He replied, "There is nothing bad on the bodily form of the conqueror. All images of this divine being are an expression

---

[72] (... continued)
temporary source of protection. The Three Jewels must be seen as the final reliance and true source of protection.

[73] Tirthikas as mentioned in the Buddhist scriptures were various types of non-Buddhist religious followers found in India. They essentially did not exist in Tibet.

of his divinity."[74] Therefore, you should train just as Atisha said. All representations, from fragments of moulded images and stupas up to complete images of the Buddha should be treated with the faith of seeing them as actual Buddha. They should be put in an elevated and clean place.

2. Starting with even a single letter, the written form of the Buddha's excellent speech should be treated with faith. Do not put such things on the bare ground or on a covered floor, either. It should not be used as a place for putting hats and clothes, and should not have other things put on it for any reason. It should not be carried together with shoes. Volumes of scripture should not be used as a shelf or support for offerings. Spit and tartar from the teeth should never touch them. These things have been taught and one should be careful about them. Sharawa said,

> Where is there any plaything in our dharma? If you do not respect dharma and those who speak it, it is a cause of losing your intelligence. Now, your current level of stupidity is sufficient; you do not need to accumulate further causes of stupidity.

Chen Ngawa said,

> It is well known that, when you come before the sacred words, you should pay homage with your palms pressed together at your heart. Seeing the body, speech, and mind representations as wealth and something to sell, that is, giving them a commercial

---

[74] This is the way of talking of ancient India where holy figures were also referred to as divinities. It means that images of the Buddha are expressions of the reality that he has realized.

value, is totally unacceptable; such attitudes should be
totally abandoned. Seeing the members of the
sangha, all the way down to the yellow robes worn
by them, as the sangha jewel should not be thought of
as a fault; you should have faith and respect for them.
Do not talk to others about faults in the sangha,
except on the specific occasions of giving instruction
about the sangha, dealing with sangha issues, and so
on.

3. Dromton Rinpoche, Ngog The Great Translator,[75] and
others said that even a strip of red or yellow cloth from a
monk's clothing that has been inserted in a cleft as rubbish,
since it has been worn as monk's clothing, cannot be taken as
not having their qualities[76]. It is said that Zhamarpa Chokyi
Wangchuk[77], when he arrived at an assembly, would prostrate

---

[75] Ngog the Translator was around at the time of Atisha. He was
a Tibetan from the district called "Ngog". He spent many years in
India and Kashmir—where the Buddha's teaching was flourishing
a that time—and became a truly expert translator. He also was a
principal disciple of Atisha and was closely involved with the
teachings of the Kadampa tradition. Thus he was also a contempo-
rary of Dromtonpa.

[76] Tibetans did not just throw out old clothes but would put them
up in a tree or a hole in a pile of rocks or a cleft in a stupa or other
such place. A tattered piece of monk's robes seen in such places is
here said to be regarded as a representation of the actual sangha
Jewel.

[77] The Zhamar line of incarnations is one of the important incarna-
tion lines of the Karma Kagyu tradition. Zhamar Chokyi
(continued ...)

to the sangha and when he left would walk out backwards so that his back was not turned to them; he would put the mat for the feast substances to his head and would lick up the remains with his tongue. And there are other stories, like that too. In particular, it is an extreme fault to denigrate others through sectarian bias, so you must not think that way. In short, you should make efforts not to accumulate any negativity with respect to the representations of body, speech, and mind and the yellow robes worn, but to venerate them with faith and sincere intent.

The five common trainings are as follows.

1. Remembering their kindness, to make offerings. With greatly respectful three doors, you should make offerings and praises, and so on. The great translator Rinchen Zangpo[78] continuously, through the six periods of day and night, made offerings to the Jewels without break. In the springtime, he told the people with him to set out the offerings at midnight. They immediately replied that it was already done and fell asleep. Then, saying to them that he would be carried off by the wind of the snores, the great translator himself went and made the offerings.

---

[77] (... continued)
Wangchuk lived from 1584–1635.

[78] Rinchen Zangpo was by far the greatest of translators of the new translation period. Both his capabilities and output were prodigious. He started his work when he was sent to Kashmir in the middle of the tenth century by the king of his areas, Lha Lama Yeshe Od. Later, he was in Tibet at the time of Atisha.

Phuchungwa[79] is reported to have said,

> At first, when you have nothing to make offerings with, continually offer the stubs of discarded, burnt incense. Later on, when your level of merit has increased, you will be able to offer the individual components of incense by themselves—duruka, agaru, and so on. Later still, you will be able to offer incense worth twenty srang[80] of gold that is made from these individual ingredients.

Dromton Rinpoche said,

> All of you have to make offerings to the Jewels now and in the future of what you have to eat and what you have to drink. If you do not, no qualities will arise in your mindstream and the ones that have arisen will degenerate.

Unequalled Dvagpo also said the same sort of thing. Je Rinpoche[81], too, said,

---

[79] Phuchungwa together with Chen Ngawa and Potowa (sometimes called Putowa) were the three main disciples of Dromtonpa and all were very important to the transmission of the Kadampa teachings.

[80] Srang was a weight measure of Tibet.

[81] Je Rinpoche refers to Tsongkhapa, who was the source of the Gelugpa tradition of Buddhist Tibet. The Kadampa tradition was incorporated into the Kagyu tradition by the Unequalled Dvagpopa, meaning Gampopa, and much later was incorporated into the Gelugpa tradition after Tsongkhapa at which time it ceased to be

(continued ...)

Through the power of roots of merit produced in relation to a holy field, the power of mind will increase. When the force of mind is extremely weak—when you listen but the words do not stick, contemplate but the meaning is not understood, meditate but the mind remains unaffected—this is an oral instruction to rely on the power of the field[82].

Neu Zur said,

By offering to the Three Jewels you will never die of hunger. By not offering to them you will never become rich.

Sharawa said,

Offering is not done with pieces of mouldy cheese or yellowing leaves, it is done with whatever is in fine condition[83].

Chen Ngawa said,

Due to having made offerings of the discarded remains of offered incense collected from the temples, we now have good things to offer. It is said, "Offer

---

[81] (... continued)
a tradition in its own right.

[82] Meaning the field of the various refuge objects, the Three Jewels in the sutras and the Three Roots in the tantras, as mentioned at the beginning of the text.

[83] He is criticizing the habit of people to make offerings to the Three Jewels with things of inferior quality.

water to the deities!", and even at that time, seven sets[84] should be offered, always. It is important that whatever you have is made into an offering to the Jewels. Nowadays for the most part people make sure that the food they eat is good and they keep some not so good food just for making offerings. Doing that has no value, it is a fault.

Glorious Karmapa[85] said,

> You can make one hundred or one thousand offerings a year of stale year-old tsampa flour and old, rancid, foul-tasting butter but this kind of virtue created from avarice and conceit has no value; it is a cause of being born as a preta.

Even if you have no wealth or possessions, do not forget to give the best portion of whatever you eat or drink. I have written some notes on the seven branches which you could look at to learn more about this way of training in making offerings to the Jewels according to the level of wealth that you possess.

2. With thoughts of compassion, leading others to take refuge. Do as much as you can, whatever you can, to establish others in taking refuge such as explaining the disadvantages of not taking refuge and the advantages of doing so, and giving the vows of refuge, and so on. If you have no-one who listens to you, not doing this is not a fault.

---

[84] Usually seven bowls of water are offered.

[85] Meaning Khakhyab Dorje, the 15th Karmapa, head of the Karma Kagyu tradition in Tibet.

3. With thoughts of the advantages, take refuge in the six periods day and night. After remembering again and again the advantages as they were explained above and the way to take refuge also as previously explained, you should do this conscientiously, day and night. When it is time to sleep, go to sleep with the refuge object invited and firmly stationed before you. When you are going somewhere, remember the buddha of that direction and go making real and imagined prostrations to him. And so on, you should at all times and in all circumstances remember the Jewels. Whether happy, whether sad, whether sick, whether pained, whether dying, whether reviving, whether good, whether bad in every case you must decisively resolve to hold to the Jewels and diligently take refuge in them.

4. With thoughts of the disadvantages, do not abandon the Jewels even if it comes to your life. At sword-point, Buddhist people were told by Muslim soldiers who had invaded ancient India and were attempting to convert everyone in the country to Islam, "Will you abandon the refuge object the Jewels or not? If you do not abandon them, I will kill you!"

In one case, an Indian named Khyeu The Joyful was seized by Tirthikas who told him, "Swear now that you will not take refuge in the Jewels! If you don't, we will kill you!" The Joyful swore that he would not abandon his refuge in the Jewels. One Tirthika said, "Die!", and drew his knife. The Joyful said, "I have been through many births and deaths. Up till now I have not met such an excellent spiritual friend as yourself! You have advised me that there is none better than Buddha and also taught me to be patient! Not only that but no-one else but you has come along who would give me in an instant a body adorned with the marks and signs because of truly overcoming grasping at a self. I really must prostrate to you and your exceptional kindness. Of all joys, today I have obtained this one: the path of seeing has been produced and there is the joy just of seeing reality as it is. Indeed, this kind of bad latency usually is very hard to defeat![86] Now you have instantly become the place of worship of all worlds of gods and men!" Joyful's joy became so great through speaking these things that the Tirthikas lost the strength of mind to kill him.

There are other stories about not relinquishing one's refuge like that one. For example, the king of Khotan was going to kill a novice Buddhist nun and a muslim from Turkey was going to kill Lha Lama Yeshe Od, however, even though it came down to their lives, they did not abandon their refuges.

A mara had convinced one king to outlaw worship of the Jewels. One nun worshipped the Jewels and made music with cymbals. The king used the wheel weapon to kill her but the music did not stop; the human music stopped but a sound of heavenly music appeared because the nun had been reborn as an incomparably beautiful goddess in the Heaven of the Thirty Three[87] and the king of the gods, Kaushika, had made her his

---

[86] After obtaining the path of insight, one immediately is stationed on the first bodhisatva level. This level is named "Utter Joy" for the fact that the person has utter joy. Moreover, it is usually very difficult to overcome the karmic seeds—latencies—that hold one back from the achievement of the level Utter Joy, yet because of these Muslim soldiers, he has suddenly overcome them and so attained utter joy.

[87] The Heaven of the Thirty-three is a realm at the top of the desire realm which has thirty-three tribes of gods in it, each with a king-like god who leads his tribe. Over all of them is Indra, who is

(continued ...)

queen. In that way giving up her life because of the Jewels became very meaningful.

Here in Tibet, there are no Tirthikas so this has not happened. Nonetheless—and let us not even talk about the many who have sworn themselves to the Jewels but abjured their oaths—there are those who see the Jewels as true and have not abjured their oaths but who, wanting to prevent some kind of negativity for themselves, have just taken an oath without actually pledging themselves to the Jewels, their parents, or whatever, and who do not actually follow on from it.

5. Without thoughts of trust, do not seek some other means. It is very important to understand that, no matter what major problems arise, it is only all right to turn to the Jewels and hold to the techniques taught by the Buddha; it is not all right to hold to the teachings of the Tirthikas or to hold to worldly gods, nagas, locale owners, and so on as a place where you can pin your hopes. If you were to pin your hopes on these others, it would be a great fault.

You can encourage yourself to take refuge in the Jewels continuously but if you do not have a firm trusting type of faith that has surrendered to the Jewels, then there is the extreme danger that, when a really major problem occurs, because of thinking that Shiva[88], gods, demons, locale owners, and so on of great power have a swifter action or greater capability than the

---

[87] (... continued)
called King of the Gods for that reason. Kaushika is the personal name of the current Indra.

[88] Shiva is another great god of the Indian Hindu religion.

Jewels, you will toss aside the Jewels and ask these other places of refuge for protection. If you do that, then you lose your vows of refuge and, because of that, the vows of individual emancipation—layman, novice, and full monk, the vows of the bodhisatva, and the vows of secret mantra, all of them, become lifeless as a corpse. Because of this, even if you observe these vows, no benefit comes of it and, later, there comes the very great problem that, because you have no place of refuge, you will not be emancipated from the sufferings of cyclic existence or the bad destinies.

You might not toss aside the Jewels but, like trying to have two things at once, might not actually trust and put your confidence in the Jewels; it is taught that, if that happens, your refuge vows have been lost. It is like trying to ride two horses at once and falling down between them. It is crucial for each of us not to forget this key point. Mara is very expert at deception and is very capable of making both sides look as though they are beneficial—but we should not be fooled by that.

In that way, you should assiduously observe the eleven vows of refuge. Importantly, if the strength of bad latencies causes you to transgress them, there is the following to be done. For the first, tenth, and eleventh of them, the refuge vows will have been completely lost. Therefore, you must immediately do a laying aside[89] with all four forces involved[90] as a support for re-taking the refuge vows. For the other eight of them, the refuge

---

[89] For laying aside, see the glossary.

[90] The four forces are the forces of support, regret, rejection, and antidote. In these, the support will be the Three Jewels, and the others are easy to understand.

vows have not been lost but have been corrupted. Therefore, you must correct those vows with full attention to the task by doing a laying aside in conjunction with the four forces.

If you observe the refuge vows like that, the benefits are inconceivable. This has already been discussed at length but to repeat it again briefly, the Buddha said that you obtain vast merit, obtain joy and supreme joy, obtain very pure samadhi, have great guardians, purify obscurations of wrong directions taken, become a holy being, please the places of refuge, give joy to the gods on the white side[91], and so on. Not only that but now all of us have obtained a human body, met the guru and precious teaching of the conqueror, and to some extent developed a mind to accomplish virtue and to abandon evil. Thus, at this point, if we exert ourselves at supplicating for refuge from the heart, then blessings will enter our mindstreams and all the good qualities of the path—faith, pure perception, renunciation, devotion, trust in karma and its effect, emptiness, compassion, and so on—will increase.

No matter what worldly activity you do, always begin it by making offerings and supplications to the Jewels. If you travel somewhere and make prostrations to the buddha of that direction, then all of your desired goals will be easily achieved. If you slough off and lose supplicating the guru and Three Jewels, then even though you have good minds of renunciation, faith, and so on, they will actually be deceptions of the learned. As has been taught, once your resolve has weakened, even if you continue in your virtuous practices, your mind will uncontrol-

---

[91] The gods on the white side are gods who are helpful to humans in general or who support the Buddha's dharma and its followers in particular.

lably turn to non-virtue. Practising generosity, observing the disciplines, meditating, and so on will just become the deluded eight worldly dharmas of this life; parents, relatives, and friends will plough you under; sickness, negative influences, and obstructions will afflict you; the obstacles of mara, wrong concepts and doubt, will appear in your mind and thereby your accumulation of virtue will be defeated. As the antidote to that, it is extremely important as all of the holy ones have unanimously said that there is nothing superior to or more profound than supplicating and taking refuge in the Jewels.

The principal thing to do in regard to this small instruction on taking refuge as it has been given above is to practise it continuously. If you would like to accumulate one hundred thousand refuges, then put your father on your right, your mother on your left, a harmful person or enemy in front, and then all sentient beings all around you. You, together with all of them, prostrate with body, take refuge with speech, and mentally prostrate with mind given over to the Jewels through the strongest faith you can muster. Do not push yourself to accumulate numbers but gradually do the practice until you have accumulated one hundred thousand of them.

More extensive presentations that explain the essential meaning, terminology, and divisions can be found in the dharmas of Maitreya[92], the texts on the bodhisatva levels[93], and the larger texts of the teachings, so, if you would like to know more,

---

[92] A set of five teachings given by Maitreya to Asanga and collectively called the Five Dharmas of Maitreya.

[93] These are texts by Asanga which clearly explain the ways of a bodhisatva.

please go to them. This presentation has been made specifically so that others like myself of smaller mental capacity can easily understand the subject, using quotations from the Buddha-Word and treatises on it adorned with the talks of the lineage gurus. The instruction just on refuge is complete at this point.

2. Trainings That are Like the Precepts of Refuge

It says in *The Section of The Bits Expressed on Need*[94],

> The path that severs the pain and misery of existence
> Will be taught to you.
> The tathagata is the teacher;
> You must do the work.

On some occasions when we are faced with harm, we are sure that we can turn it away and protect ourselves from it. However, to get protection from all other circumstances, that is, every one of the sufferings of cyclic existence and the bad states, requires the following. First, we diligently surrender to the Jewels and take refuge in them. When we do that, blessings do enter the mind and through that, the mind of dharma gradually increases and the mind of evil gradually decreases. Then, the ways of adopting virtue and relinquishing evil become stronger and we journey by stages through the levels and paths until we attain complete enlightenment. At that time, it is said, we have completed or finished the refuge.

The dharma lord Neu Zur said,

> Having taken refuge in the holy places of refuge, we
> might wonder how much protection they will afford?
> Protection is provided by the dharma. How does the
> dharma protect? It protects from the sufferings of the

---

[94] This is one of the twelve sections of the sutras.

world that come from seeking just the purposes of this life through meditation on the recollection of death. It protects from the entirety of the suffering of cyclic existence through the path of the middling being and the three trainings that go with it. It protects from the Lesser Vehicle by the path of the superior being and the method and prajna that go with it.[95]

Thus, the method of protection shown by the teacher, the Buddha, is the dharma. The sangha, the ones who are established on the path, know the way to practise it, and we too must train in it to the extent that we are capable. That way of practice is extremely vast but, in brief, it is as follows. There are two vehicles, the Lesser and Greater vehicles. The former has in it the dharma teachings of the lesser and middling beings; this system in which one journeys only for oneself is not widespread here in Tibet. The latter, the Greater Vehicle, also has in it the two vehicles of sutra and tantra; the former exists as a widely known system of training passed on through the lineage of Glorious Dipankara that still has its blessings and explanations intact and the latter is the training in mantra which is done as Kriyatantra, Charyatantra, and Yogatantra. The last of the three has an inner level of training, Unsurpassed Yogatantra, within which Father Tantra is trained in as

---

[95] This is a summary of the complete path of sutra dharma as taught by the Kadampas in their Stages of the Path teaching. The teaching explains the dharma through what it called "the three beings". The least type of being does no more than close the door to births in the bad destinies. The middling being aims for personal emancipation from cyclic existence. The great being aims for true complete enlightenment.

Mahayoga; Mother Tantra is trained in as Anuyoga; and Non-Dual Tantra is trained in as Atiyoga[96]. Furthermore, in Atiyoga, there is the outer level which is trained in as Mind Section Mahamudra, there is the inner level which is trained in as Space Section, and there is the secret level which is trained in as Foremost Instruction Section. These trainings are entered through instruction in the dharma doors appropriate to each one that is obtained from a fully-qualified spiritual friend whose mind has already been trained in that system. By attending the holy ones, wrong understandings are eliminated through hearing, certainty is gained through contemplation, and finality is obtained through meditation.

Then I have this comment to make to myself:

> When arousing faith in the attainment of a human
>   body of freedom and endowment,
> If like a blind man grabbing the tail of an elephant
>   and not letting go,
> You make effort at taking refuge in the non-deceptive
>   guardians,
> You will accomplish great goals without difficulty.

> That being so, what could happen from listening
> To an irrelevant person like myself?
> Therefore, I henceforth must
> Without doubts be assiduous at the three.

---

[96] The newer translation schools simply train in father, mother, or non-dual tantra forms of Unsurpassed Yogatantra. The older translation school, which is contained in the Nyingma teachings, trains in them in the way stated here.

This small instruction on taking refuge, called "The Great Entrance to the Excellent House of the Conqueror's Precious Teaching" was written in the mountain area called Mandong in the Earth Female Ox Year by the old monk and reciter of the mani, Ngedon Tengyay, who is sustained under the refuge of the guru Holder of The Lotus, Glorious Karmapa, and the holders of his lineage. The seeker of virtue Master of Offerings Phunstog requested me repeatedly to put in writing something that could be used for meditation and some laypeople with faith also expressed their hope for the same, but this was mainly written to refresh my memory. I dedicate it so that all the motherly sentient beings may quickly be held within the refuge of the Jewels.

From the Stages of the Path
To Enlightenment:

For Beginners in the Great Vehicle, The Method of Meditating on Compassion That References Sentient Beings Called "An Ornament for the Minds Of Young Conquerors' Sons"

Namo guru mahakarunikaya[97]

> The Holder of the White Lotus[98] who embodies in
> one person the love of all conquerors,
> Who, unblinking, looks continuously on migrators
> And lives as a member of the saffron order[99] for the
> benefit of myself and others;

---

[97] This says, "Homage to the guru, the body of great compassion."

[98] The Holder of the White Lotus is Avalokiteshvara in the form of Karmapa.

[99] The saffron order is the ordained Buddhist sangha, whose robes were originally white muslin died in left-over saffron liquid.

Chief of all places of refuge, the guru, together with
    his sons
From my heart I bow in homage and take refuge in
    you.
I bow down to all, noble and ordinary beings,
Who possess the two enlightenment minds[100].
The root of the Great Vehicle, sutra and tantra, is
    compassion
And the beginner's way of meditating on it is
A style of meditation that takes sentient beings as its
    reference,
So I will write about that here in this ornament for
    the minds of young conquerors' sons
To benefit myself and others like me;
Holder of the Lotus, please bless my mindstream.

Now, the root of the Great Vehicle is the enlightenment mind
and nothing else. If you do not have it, then, even if you have
developed the ability through the practices of development
stage, winds and channels, and so on to manifest a body of fire

---

[100] For enlightenment mind, see the glossary. The two enlightenment minds are the fictional and superior factual types of enlightenment mind. For fictional and superior factual see the glossary.
The fictional type of enlightenment mind is the conventional type.
It is explained as consisting of love and great compassion within
the framework of an intention to obtain true complete enlightenment for the sake of all sentient beings. The superior fact truth is
the ultimate type. It is explained as the enlightenment mind which
is directly perceiving emptiness. Fictional and superior factual
have been translated as "relative" and "absolute" respectively for
many years but those translations are totally mistaken.

or water or to manifest wild beasts, and so on, or even if you have the ability to fly in the sky, or even if, through having obtained the qualities of the four absorptions[101], you have the extra-sensory perceptions which allow you to see the details of hundreds of lifetimes, you will not be able to attain buddhahood through it. The Tirthika yogins have many of these attainments too, but do not become emancipated through them.

If you do not have enlightenment mind, no matter how much you practise the virtues of generosity, discipline, and so on, buddhahood will not be attained, and not only that, even if you have the realized the supreme quality, emptiness, if you have not aroused compassion, the ultimate will not be realised. You might develop a partial realization but, without compassion, you will not go beyond the simple emancipation that comes with it, on to buddhahood. For example, if you want the autumn harvest, the springtime seeds must be planted; without planting the seeds, you might toil throughout the summer months, doing the farm work of watering, manuring, and so on, but a harvest cannot come from it. Similarly, if enlightenment mind—which is like the seed—is not present, then no matter how much virtuous action—which is like the water and manure—you do, the happiness of cyclic existence or the simple emancipation of the shravakas and pratyekabuddhas will be possible but the attainment of true complete buddhahood will not. Therefore, it is extremely important to exert yourself at the methods for arousing the root of the attainment of buddhahood, which is enlightenment mind.

---

[101] These are the four absorptions that correspond to the four levels of the formless realm. Attainment of these absorptions brings the attainment of many supernormal capacities of mind.

Yang Gon Rinpoche[102] said, "The reality called Dzogchen is of no benefit in itself, the person must become Dzogchen." Similarly, the teaching called Great Vehicle is of no benefit in itself, the person must enter and engage in the Great Vehicle. If a person has aroused enlightenment mind, then he has entered into the Great Vehicle. The *Great Stages of the Path*[103] sets down the following as an extremely key point: "When enlightenment mind is just mere words, understanding, or intent, then the secret mantra part of the Great Vehicle also becomes just mere words, understanding, or intent, but when enlightenment mind becomes real enlightenment mind, then the Great Vehicle also becomes the real Great Vehicle."

This enlightenment mind, moreover, consists of two types: fictional enlightenment mind and superior fact enlightenment mind. The former corresponds to compassion and the latter to emptiness. It is said that all of the virtuous practices that a person who is practising to attain buddhahood does—accumulation of merit, purification of obscuration, and so on—are techniques for producing these two. Moreover, unless the two are finally unified as one, there is no becoming a buddha. Nonetheless, beginners have to start by training in the fictional enlightenment mind.

The sovereign of the enlightenment mind teachings, Jowo Je Atisha, said, "If you do not know how to train in enlightenment mind, it will not be produced." So, training is necessary.

---

[102] A famous early master of the Drukpa Kagyu.

[103] One of Tsongkhapa's main works. It was, at its time, the most extensive presentation of the Kadampa Stages of the Path teaching ever made.

But which system of training should you use? Atisha said that it is necessary to train gradually in the foremost instructions that set out the five or seven causes and effects. Atisha explained the five causes and effects like this: "If you want the effect of being a buddha, then you must have its cause which is enlightenment mind. If you want the effect which is enlightenment mind, then you must have its cause, great compassion for all sentient beings. If you want the effect which is great compassion, then you must have its cause which is loving kindness that delights in all sentient beings. If you want the effect which is delighted loving kindness, then you must have its cause which is to feel the kindness of sentient beings. If you want the effect which is to feel their kindness, then you must have its cause which is knowing that all sentient beings are mother and father."

Atisha said that the key points should be understood like this,

> If you first understand that all sentient beings are
> mother and father, then its effect, a feeling of their
> kindness, is easy to produce. If you have a feeling for
> their kindness, it is easy to produce delighted loving
> kindness. If you have produced delighted loving
> kindness, compassion is easy to produce. If you have
> produced compassion, enlightenment mind is easy to
> produce. If you have produced enlightenment mind,
> the attainment of buddhahood is easy.

Adding to that, Atisha said this,

> Generally speaking, if you think again and again
> about the sufferings of those sentient beings, you will
> give rise to a mind that wishes just for them to be free
> from their sufferings. Nonetheless, that mind has to
> be produced strongly and firmly. To do so, it is first

necessary to have a mind of exceptional loving kindness that delights in and cherishes sentient beings, like a mother has for an only child or an animal has for its beloved offspring. Ordinarily, if suffering arises for those held as close, unbearable compassion for them will arise but if suffering arises for those seen as an enemy, the unbearable feeling of compassion is put to one side. The difference is whether or not one takes joy in others, that is, it is the difference between having a mind that does and does not take delight in others. If suffering arises for all those held as neither close nor distant, who are seen as in-between, then there is neither thought of joy nor sadness and the mind perceives all of them with neither delight nor aversion.

Those who benefit you bring joy to your mind and therefore are attractive to you so, when suffering arises for them, an unbearable concern for them immediately appears in your mind. That is the reason why having a feeling for the kindness of sentient beings is necessary when producing delight in them. Here, the key point in the production of a feeling for their kindness is that the most kind ones are motherly types, therefore, it is necessary to understand that all sentient beings have been one's father and mother at one time or another.

If you have given rise to some understanding of how difficult freedom and endowment are to obtain, of death and impermanence, of karma and effect, of the disadvantages of cyclic existence, and so on, as shown in the Stages of the Path literature, and then you give rise to each of the experiences as they should be produced according to this training of understanding sentient beings as mother, developing a feeling for their kindness, developing delighted loving kindness, developing compassion, and developing enlightenment mind, then that is extremely good. However, for those who have not managed to do that, here is a brief description of the meditation system.

In this meditation system, there are five topics—recognising that all beings have been one's mother, remembering their kindness, developing loving kindness, developing compassion, and then arousing enlightenment mind. It says in all of the sutras, tantras, and treatises on them that the root of dharma is compassion, because when compassion has been produced, enlightenment mind comes about itself without need of exertion. Therefore, compassion becomes the chief thing to meditate on and in that case, the three of recognising mother, remembering the kindness, and loving kindness become the techniques that are the causes for producing compassion.

Compassion is the main meditation here and the other four parts of recognising all beings have been mother, remembering their kindness, developing loving kindness, and arousing the enlightenment mind become ancillaries to it. This whole meditation is then explained in three parts: the preliminaries, the main part, and a discussion of related items.

1. PRELIMINARIES:

There are two parts:

1. The common preliminaries
2. The preliminaries of this system of instruction

1. The Common Preliminaries

Kongtrul Rinpoche has said that at the beginning of every session, the verse of refuge and arousing the enlightenment mind should be said three times while recollecting the meaning:

> I take refuge in the buddha, dharma, and supreme
>   assembly
> Until enlightenment is attained;
> By my merits of practising giving and the others,
> May I accomplish buddhahood for the sake of
>   migrators.

Having done that, your attention should be directed to guru Avalokiteshvara, the embodiment of all places of refuge, seated above the crown of your head on a lotus-moon seat, and then, with intense faith and devotion, you should say the following:

> Authentic guru, great spiritual friend competent in all
>   teachings, please grant me your blessings;
> Please give rise to especially good loving-kindness,
>   compassion, and enlightenment mind in my
>   mindstream.

At the end of saying that however many times, think that the guru descends into you through your Brahma Aperture and remains seated in an egg-shaped pavilion of light at your heart. Practise devotion.

2. The Preliminaries of this System of Instruction

Think like this. "Oh my! Now I have obtained a human body with freedom and endowment, have met the Buddha's teachings, have met many gurus and heard the holy dharma from them, have understood virtue and evil, yet at this time, when I do have some freedom to choose, my life's actions are not profitable but entail a great loss, like poisoned food. My activity is an endless procession of things coming and going like ripples on water. All that I do is meaningless, like a dream, like an illusion. I will not allow myself to be pre-occupied by this kind of action any longer; through the whole succession of my lives I must diligently work at virtue, which is truly beneficial. Even then, it is taught that this is not necessarily beneficial to my mind; when outwardly virtuous actions turn into the assistants of inward affliction, they just serve to replenish my collection of evil deeds. Thus, I must do one dharma which will benefit this mind of mine. Moreover, I must exert myself at the root of the attainment of buddhahood, the very heart of every dharma teaching, the two types of precious enlightenment mind. Moreover, I must exert myself at the meditation on the exceptionally beneficial yet easy for laypeople to understand dharma, the root of the fictional enlightenment mind, compassion. And moreover, I should be quick about it. The time of death is not definite."

Thinking about the human condition, you see that, up until now, every single person—high, low, and in-between; enemy, friend, and in-between; close, distant, and in-between; old, young, and in-between—has died. Who knows whether the next month or the next life will come first? None of us knows the time of death. Death itself is a small thing compared to the fact that, after death, we are driven on by the force of karma with no control over where we will be born.

If you look at karma, we humans have many evil ones and few virtuous ones, so we could easily be born in the bad destinies that are truly fearsome: the heat and cold of the hells; the hunger and thirst of the pretas; and the dumbness and stupidity of the animals. Then there is the strife and fighting of the asuras; the transference and fall at death of the gods; and the birth, old age, sickness, death, poverty, taxes and debts[104], the mental anguish of the upper classes of humans and physical suffering of the lower classes of humans. No matter where anyone is born in the six classes of beings in the various abodes of cyclic existence, it is the nature of suffering. Suffering blazes like a fire, rages like water, bears down like mountains. Wherever you dwell it becomes a helper and ally of suffering. Whatever body you take, it is a body of suffering. Whatever your possessions, they are the possessions of suffering. Whatever sensations you have, they are the sensations of suffering.

All suffering sensations are the suffering of suffering—for example, like eating poisoned food and becoming sick because of it. All pleasant sensations are changeable suffering—for example, like eating good food then adding poison to it and eating that. All neutral sensations—the ones which have neither factor of being pleasant nor unpleasant—are the suffering of formatives[105]; this is like eating poisoned food has no degree to

---

[104] Tibetans were (and still are at the time of writing) often faced with extreme taxes—the situation was similar to the baronies of medieval Europe. And then, in general, many had to borrow money to keep going.

[105] The Buddha taught three sufferings: suffering of suffering, suffering of change, and suffering of the formatives. The latter is the fact that sentient beings have the fourth aggregate, the aggregate of the formatives, which is the deep cause of continuing on into further samsaric existences. Formatives are so-called because they cause the formation of future sets of aggregates in future existence. When you have this aggregate, you are already poisoned
(continued ...)

it—you are poisoned. There is no distinction at all in these three sufferings except possibly to say that one precedes, goes a little deeper than another.

There is no fundamental difference between going up to birth in a god realm and falling down into the hells. Going into these abodes of cyclic existence is like going into a house ablaze with fire; unless you free yourself and escape from it through a window, door, or some other exit, how could you possibly rest at ease? Being in this cyclic existence is like the merchants who went to the cannibal demoness's island[106]. Therefore, decide clearly that any attachment to the happiness within cyclic existence is just the cause of ruin, even for lay people[107]. Being in this cyclic existence is like being imprisoned in a swirling, filthy toilet vast as an ocean. Except for wondering when you could possibly be released from this situation that you have mistakenly fallen into because of helpless attachment to it, how could you possibly think of any part of it as a festive occasion let alone see it as a place in which you would want to stay?

We have confused the suffering nature of cyclic existence with happiness and, having done that, have lost our minds to and become attached to wealth and possessions; family and friends; personal gain and position; clothes, jewellery, and material

---

[105] (... continued)
and everything you do contributes to the death of samsaric existence.

[106] In the sutras, the story is told of merchants who thought that undertaking a difficult sea voyage would result in great rewards, but the voyage ended up being misery from beginning to end.

[107] It is ruin for monks and nuns and equally so for laypeople.

things; fame and respect; offerings from our students, and so on. All of these are confused appearances. All of them entertain, occupy, and fool us and in doing so have the very big fault that they help us to accumulate bad actions. It is our minds seeing things the wrong way around because of our karmic obscurations; for example, insects do not go to valuable things like wish-fulfilling jewels but swarm around filth because of their mistaken minds. Therefore you should think, "Now I must exert myself at laying aside the previously done evil, the causes I have for suffering in cyclic existence, and henceforth must abandon these like I would poison. Even lower people in society think that they should look on themselves with compassion and take care of their own situations, so I will abandon the evil deeds that I can and for those that I cannot, I will regret them, lay them aside, and make an aspiration from my heart to be able to abandon them in future." You must produce virtue for yourself which, like medicine, is the cause of release from cyclic existence and moreover, you must accumulate it like those who want material things, not being satisfied with what you have already and not dawdling over it.

Think again and again, "I must be diligent in taking refuge with all my being in the guru and Three Jewels, the ones who protect us from the sufferings of cyclic existence", then put into practise whatever practices you can. This is important: it is said, "If you take joy in cyclic existence as you take joy in arriving at a temple[108], and are attached to it, there is no way that you will be able to arouse compassion for the sentient beings wandering in cyclic existence. We laypeople who are socially in the lower classes do not have the good fortune of being able to turn away

---

[108] Ordinary Tibetans are overwhelmed with faith just on arriving at a Buddhist shrine of any sort.

attachment to the seemingly-pleasant appearances of cyclic existence, but if we do not stop seeing good in those things and start seeing the faults in them, then no matter what virtue we produce, it has been said that it will not have a great effect on our journey to emancipation. And for that reason, it is also said that it is a major key point to understand that the happy aspects of cyclic existence are faulty. That is true for householders, but especially true for those who wear the yellow robes; for them it is a major fault not to stop looking at the happiness, food, clothes, talk, and so on of cyclic existence.

At the end of each session, do these dedications and prayers of aspiration.

> By these roots of merit of mine, may I attain the level
> of a buddha for the sake of all sentient beings. In
> general, may I become able to lead every sentient
> being by myself alone to the level of a buddha.
> Particularly, from this time until buddhahood is
> obtained and even while dreaming, may I not forget
> the two types of precious enlightenment mind, and
> may they develop further and further. May I be able
> to turn whatever bad circumstances arise into the
> assistants of enlightenment mind.

And,

> Mañjuśhrī knows how it is and is heroic
> And Samantabhadra is like that too;
> Following them in every way, I train and
> Will utterly dedicate all of these virtues.

And others, whichever ones you know.

Between sessions, remember again and again whatever it was that you just meditated on and make efforts to amass the accumulations and purify the obscurations. Recite *Reciting the Names of Manjushri, Diamond Cutter Prajnaparamita Sutra, The King of Prayers of Aspiration, The Prayer for Excellent Conduct,* and so on and even if you do not know those, it is said to be very important to make efforts at reciting the names of the bodhisatvas and especially the seven limbs (I have composed a text called *The Treasury, A Perfect Collection of Commentaries* which will help to understand the meaning of the seven limbs)[109]. In sessions, if you meditate on and recite the mani, that is good.

In that way, do the refuge and enlightenment mind supplications at the opening of a session and the dedications and aspirations to conclude it. All the rest required for a session is done within that as the container.

2. THE MAIN PART

The main part is meditation on compassion. There are three types of compassion: compassion in reference to sentient beings; compassion in reference to the dharma; and compassion without reference. Here, the method of meditating on compassion with reference to sentient beings will be explained. It is in ten parts.

1. The object of meditation on compassion, all sentient beings, seen as father and mother

At the opening of a session, take refuge and arouse enlightenment mind, and so on as explained above, then do following.

---

[109] This is a text of the Mandong Hermit which has not been translated into English at the time of writing.

Think, "It is said in the Buddha Word and all of the treatises on it[110] that I have been born and born and died and died without beginning in the abodes of cyclic existence because of which there is not one single sentient being alive now who has not been my father or mother. I do not know this directly because I do not have the higher perceptions, but there cannot be any falsehoods in the words of the omniscient Buddha, therefore all sentient beings have been fathers and mothers of mine." Come to a firm decision about it.

Think from deep down, "Fathers and mothers are extremely kind, therefore all sentient beings also have been kind", and then make a definite decision that all sentient beings have been kind fathers and mothers. Having done that, think that all sentient beings however many are seen, however many are heard, also have been your kind fathers and mothers. Once the decision has been made, you should familiarise yourself continuously with this thought that they have been your fathers and mothers.

At the conclusion of the session, do the dedications, as discussed above.

One major key point is apparent here. If you have produced a mind that genuinely thinks that all of them—except perhaps for a few of the worst ones—have been your fathers and mothers who should not be harmed but should be helped, you will trip yourself up with many bad types of conduct and the virtues produced through this kind of mind will not be fully beneficial.

---

[110] The Buddha Word here refers to the recorded discourses of the Buddha and the treatises on it refers to the treatises of great masters, mainly Indians, that were written to support it.

2. Meditation on compassion for the kindest one, the mother of this life

Well, just how kind have all of these sentient beings been? They have been just as kind as the father and mother of this life, that is how kind they are.

Now, for the kindness of this life's mother. Think, "The kindness of this life's mother is clear to me through my own mother; this motherly woman has been extremely kind to me. First, for over nine months she held me inside her body. And during that time, she thought, "I must do all that I can to ensure that this child of mine does not die, musn't I?" She held me dearer than her own life. She gave me a human life, body, and the opportunities that go with it. When I came out of her, I was completely helpless, unable to do anything, like a bug! But then a bug has some capability to move about, so in fact, I was even more helpless than a bug! If my mother had not looked out for me, I would have died within the day, but, without placing any importance on herself, she did not reject me but served me humbly. She supported me with her own hands, warmed me with the heat of her own body, put my mouth to her nipples, pressed milk from her breasts with her own hands, and had her sleep broken at night because of concern for me. Then, when I could swallow whole food a little, she gave up the best food to me, blew on it out of concern that it would burn my mouth, spoon fed me, cleaned up my messes with her own hands, and sucked the snot from my nose[111]. Whatever was a problem for me she took completely as her own problem and tried to find

---

[111] Western mothers wipe their children's noses. Tibetan mothers sometimes suck the snot from their children's noses.

a way to solve it. She cared for me with a loving mind. She looked at me with the eyes of loving kindness. She spoke sweet words to me. Even when there was no cause for praise, she praised me. She said all sorts of sweet things to me, even when I could not understand or respond. She kept my mind happy using many different methods. When I cried, her heart pounded with thoughts of concern; what is it—was I sick, was I hurt, was I dying? When she was worried that I was sick or dying she sought divinations, prognostications, medicine, religious workers, and helpers of all kinds who used their various methods to keep me alive and well. She used all the known methods for keeping me happy, bouncing me up and down, talking to me, and so on. She made many prayers of aspiration for me, so that I would have a long life, not be sick, be wealthy, be successful, and so on. When I was bigger, she would give me anything she had, without thought of loss, and, on top of that, with a happy mind. There was nothing I needed she would not give me. She gave up her food, her drink, her clothes for me, she gave up her possessions for the sake of my happiness in this life and she took the time to make offerings for my welfare in future lives. She nurtured her child without concern either for this life or future lives and in doing so, did not always create a happy or dharmically useful future for herself. She would even do evils and non-virtues on my behalf. She suffered in various ways because of tirelessly looking after me—her hands like wood, feet like stone, legs tired out from running around, cold under the stars at night and freezing on the frosty winter mornings[112]—but she exerted herself enormously and still gave whatever she had. That is how much this motherly being nurtured me with love. That is how much difficulty she went through and how much

---

[112] The lives of many Tibetans, for example the nomads, are like that.

she toiled to look after me. That is how great was her kindness to me. That is how much she helped me. And it said that it is not only this one time now but that she has been my mother and father through countless numbers of births and in each one of them she has helped me in the same way as she has now. If all of the milk drunk from her nipple and all the tears that she had shed on my behalf were pooled, it would be larger than the biggest ocean, it is said. Whatever was tasty, she gave to me. Whatever was soft, she dressed me in. What possible way could there be to return the kindness of this kind person? Therefore the Buddha himself said, "Even if you were to serve your parents by carrying them around the world on your shoulders, it could not return their kindness."

Think, "On my account and without regard for evil deeds done or sufferings experienced, this woman will go on to experience various sufferings in cyclic existence. How I feel compassion for her!" Turn your mind to the evil deeds and sufferings of your mother and meditate on compassion.

Think like this, "If I think about my current mother, this motherly woman would, without regard for her own evil deeds or sufferings, do anything for me. At the moment, she is subject to all the troubles of sickness, old age, and death. And my goodness, after this life's sickness and death, since she has uncountable numbers of evil deeds and will have no ability to increase her virtue, she might fall into the bad states in her next life where this kind mother of mine will have to experience all sorts of different sufferings. How I have compassion for her!" Then meditate on that.

"If I think about my mothers who are not my current mother, they have nurtured me with the same level of kindness and these motherly ones have, because of me, accumulated uncountable evil deeds. They have no opportunity to increase their virtue. They experience the three sufferings of sickness, old age, and death. I have no idea where they are now. If they have fallen into the bad states, they are experiencing suffering that I could not bear to experience! I wonder, is that what is happening to them? If that is what has happened, then how I have compassion for these mothers of mine! How awful for them!" Think like that.

To sum up, remember the evil deeds and sufferings of mothers and meditate on compassion until it can bring tears dripping from your eyes. Then, make this supplication intensely: "Guru, Three Jewels, and yidam Avalokitesvhara look here! Please purify the evil deeds of these kind mothers of mine and alleviate all of their sufferings! Please make sure that all of my virtue is obtained by my mothers!" It is easy to arouse this, so bring on the experience of it and meditate on that so that you become certain of it. If the experiences are not aroused for you by this, then understand that they also will not be aroused for anybody else, so you should work assiduously at this, it is said.

3. The end of that, meditation on great kindness as a whole

A father's kindness is usually like a mother's kindness, so meditate on that in the same kind of way. Furthermore, close relatives, close friends, and so on—all those whom you see as having a greater level of kindness—have been, if you think about it from the perspective of a beginningless succession of lives, just as kind to you as your mother of this life. There is no difference in the help that they have provided. They also are none other than kind, motherly beings. And in this life, too, they do this and that to help us. Think about how they have been kind by doing this and that and, remembering the full extent of how they have helped you, meditate on strong compassion for their evil deeds and sufferings, then do the refuge supplication and dedicate your virtues as above.

Then, it says to meditate on the greater sufferings, as follows.

4. Meditation on sentient beings in the hells

All of the sentient beings experiencing the sufferings of hell are none other than the kind fathers and mothers of mine. How I feel compassion for them! The ground and all of the mountains and rivers of the hot hells are red-hot burning iron. These places burn continuously with a fire that is like seven fires at once and with flames a cubit high. In one hell, there are many weapons that cut the inhabitants' bodies into pieces, and when the beings have died, the words "you are revived" come from the sky and they are revived again only to be killed again. They have to die and be revived again like this ten thousand times a day. Some are stretched out on top of the burning iron ground, their limbs stretched in the four directions and pegged with iron stakes. Many black lines are drawn on their bodies in a latticework and then saws cut, knives butcher, awls pierce, axes hack, chisels gouge, and spears penetrate their bodies. While the bottom part is being carved up, the top is being set up, and while the top is being carved up, the bottom is being set up. When that is done, the whole remains are cut to pieces till nothing is left. Some are gathered together in hundreds, thousands, ten of thousands, or hundreds of thousands on top of the burning iron ground, then a giant hammer the size of a mountain is raised up into the sky and smashes down on all of them. They scream and are reduced to a mess of blood and bones which turns into a river of blood that flows away. The hammer is raised again, each being becomes whole again, and the cycle repeats. Some are in a burning iron house where their whole carcass is slowly roasted from red to black. Some are impaled on burning iron spears that are pushed in through the head to stick out from the anus and when that is done, the spears are pushed through in reverse. The whole body is on fire and fire and smoke pour out from all the holes of the body. Some are burning inside and out with cracking sounds as the bones in their legs split apart and with terrible shrieking sounds because of their pain—the fire and the beings cannot be distinguished. Some have their tongues stretched out over an enormous plain and their tongues are then ploughed through with burning iron ploughs into five hundred or so furrows. Some are boiled like rice and beans in giant iron cauldrons. Some are flat on the burning iron ground and are rolled up in the hot iron. Some have molten iron poured into their mouths burning their mouths and all of their innards. Some have one thousand iron nails knocked into them.[113]

Some are put into a filthy mire where many insects with copper beaks and iron beaks bore holes into and eat them till they are like sieves. Some are chased by fierce beasts up Shalmali trees where many iron thorns with sixteen spikes each pierce their bodies, cutting them to shreds. Then birds with iron beaks dig out their eyes and pick out their brains. Some are put into the pit of live embers where they sink into the burning fire up to the knees or waists and are totally burned. Some are on the road of razors where, every time they take a step, their feet are slashed into pieces. When they lift the foot again, it is healed again. Some have their bodies cut to pieces by a rain of swords. Some have their bodies cooked in a river of hot ashes till the flesh falls off the bones which are cooked white and, their consciousness still present, they float to the surface; their flesh

----

[113] This has been a description of the eight great hot hells.

regenerates, they sink into the river where they are cooked again till the flesh falls off their bones, and so on, again and again.[114]

In the dim wastelands of the cold hells, some in raging blizzards of snow and ice have their bodies so frozen that they become ice through and through. Some have blisters on their bodies burst open, then pus and blood drips from the wounds, and freezing into ice, it pierces them. Some, in hells even colder than that, cry out with words, "It's cold!" Others in hells even colder than that cannot even speak intelligible words, they just moan "Oh, Oh." Others in hells even colder than that cannot utter any sound but simply have their teeth chattering while they quiver with cold. Others in hells even colder than that have their bodies crack open into four and eight parts. Others in hells even colder than that have their bodies crack into one hundred thousand parts and the bones, muscles, and other parts of the flesh all become indistinct.[115]

All of the beings described above experience extreme suffering but cannot die a final death. They cry out the names of those they were close to—mother, father, siblings, relatives, and close friends, and they scream out in pain and weep in misery. How I feel for all of them who have been mother and father who were nothing but kind. How awful for them.

Before, because of concern that my mouth would be burned, my mother blew on hot food and drink before giving it to me. When I was small and trying to eat a large piece of meat, I

---

[114] This has been a description of the neighbouring hells.

[115] This has been a description of the eight great cold hells.

would cut my small hands with the knife and upon asking "Mother, please help me to cut it", she would cut it and give it to me. If a small thorn stuck into me, she would help me to remove it. Out of concern that I would become cold, she put me inside her clothes and kept me warm with her body heat. These motherly ones who treated me as their own heart now are having to experience these sufferings of heat and cold. How I feel compassion for them! How sad I feel at this.

The Buddha said, "If the body of one person had three hundred or so spears stuck into it in one day, the suffering would be very great indeed but this is a small suffering that does not compare with the suffering of the hells." If that kind of intense suffering happened to me, I could not take even a hundredth, not even a thousandth fraction of it. If I could not stand it at all, how could these motherly ones stand it? They could not stand it! But they have no control and have to experience these kinds of suffering! How I feel compassion for them! Oh how I am concerned for them!

The Buddha said that their hellish sufferings do not last for one day, not for one month, not for one year, one hundred years, one thousand years, ten thousand years, one hundred thousand, one million, ten million, or one hundred million years, but have to be experienced for a length of time which cannot be calculated in this world. Oh! How sad that is! I have no ability to help them and neither do those greater than I, such as the gods Brahma and Vishnu.

With that in mind, say the following and other such words to take refuge and supplicate from the depths of your heart. "Guru, Three Jewels, and yidam deity Great Compassionate

One[116] look here! Protect these suffering mothers of mine! Look over them! Please make sure that these suffering mothers of mine receive all my virtues of the three times. Please release them from the sufferings of the hot and cold hells."

If those of lesser capability were to take this section bit by bit and do this refuge and supplication with each part again and again, it would be good. It is said that if you are alone, that it is good to do these refuge supplications out aloud.

5. Meditation on sentient beings who are pretas

The sentient beings experiencing the pretas' sufferings of hunger and thirst also are none other than the kind fathers and mothers of mine. How I feel compassion for them! They are doomed to hunger and thirst for many hundreds of thousands of years. They do not find so much as one drop of water to drink. Their bodies are so emaciated that the bones stick out of their skin. Their mouths are as dry as a bone. Their heads have no covering of hair so they are chilled by the winter sun and burned by the summer moon. Falling rain always appears as a shower of fire to them. Some see a pile of food in the distance; they go to it with their tongues hanging out, driving themselves on and on, exhausted, and when they arrive the food either turns into a rainbow image or is guarded by many fierce demons brandishing weapons so that, no matter which direction they come from, even though they can see the food, they cannot get at it to eat. Even hungrier and more thirsty than before, some cannot move their limbs. Others see a river and, though they cannot move properly, drive themselves on and on until they arrive, but when they do arrive, the river disappears

---

[116] Avalokiteshvara.

into the ground. As thirsty as they are, there is no moisture to be had anywhere. Thinking, "Where am I, what is this place?", they stretch out their hands, put their ears to the ground and listen. Their hunger, thirst, and mental suffering is very great indeed. Some have bellies bigger even than a tent or house. Their throats are thin as needles and their mouths are even smaller than the eye of the needle so, even if they do find food or drink, because no relief is possible through their mouths, their suffering is exceptionally great. Some have to eat things that only cause suffering—filth, pus and blood, fire, and so on, and, when they eat it, it turns to fire and burning iron, and their mouths and innards are burned and they suffer more than being burned by fire. Moreover, all of these beings experiencing these various sufferings are my kind mothers who nurtured me again and again with sweet breast milk, who gave me all different types of tasty food, who gave me soft clothes to wear. Right now these beings have wretched bodies which must experience these kinds of suffering. How I do have compassion for them. How I feel sad for them! It is awful this great suffering of theirs!

How long does this go on for? The Buddha said it usually lasts for fifteen thousand of their years. For me now, if I go without food for a day, I feel my mouth again and again as an empty cavern so how could I deal with their suffering of hunger?

You should take refuge with "Guru, Three Jewels, and ..." and supplicate intensely as above but use "Please act to release the pretas from their sufferings of hunger and thirst ..."

6. Meditation on sentient beings who are animals

The sentient beings who are animals also are none other than fathers and mothers of mine. How I have compassion for these ones with their various sufferings!

It is said, "There is a vast ocean at the fringes[117], filled with organisms and food. The smallest ones are as minute as the tip of a needle and even smaller again. The largest ones are as big as the mountain range that stretches between Lhasa and Samye." The largest ones could drink the ocean in a gulp, the smallest ones would need innumerable sips. The smallest ones, uncountable in number, eat the larger ones by penetrating them and slowly eating them apart. They are carried about by the ocean currents. They have no place of refuge. They go in a state of fear and suffering.

There are dark worlds where the inhabiting animals do not see the way; they stumble and fall over the edges of precipices. They eat each other. Some eat themselves and, not realizing what they are doing, continue to eat.

There are insects amongst humans. They are born by the warmth of the sun and many die again the same day. They are squashed by humans and larger animals alike and die.

Deer and similar animals live in fear of enemies appearing; they have no peace of mind. They like to eat in grassy places but even then they eat in a state of unease and fear. Being thirsty they go to the river; if things go well they drink a little in fear, if things do not go well, there is the sound of a gunshot and a bullet through the heart kills one of them. Like this, they live in fear throughout their years while we men kill them as though they were enemies in war. The others run off in panic but never have the nerve to go down to drink from the river again. Thirsty, they travel on in a weakened state. Some are chased by men with many dogs and, panicking, lie low in rocky

---

[117] Meaning at the fringes of the land mass.

crags. Some get caught in traps and snares. Then they have a gun fired at them and are killed. Until they actually die, can you imagine the level of their fear? If another person were to set us up as their target and then fire a gun at us, what level of fear would that produce in us? How much compassion I have for beings like this!

The ones who are dying—ones who have been my fathers and mothers—are watched helplessly by the animals who are their parents. When they were calves, baby goats, lambs, and so on, they drank the sweet milk of their mothers and lay there helplessly while they were kept corralled by their human owners. When they could move, they were separated from their mothers and taken elsewhere or were tied together with others. Not only that but the males, seen as less valuable and called "useless", were put aside and treated worse. How much sickness and suffering do they have? If we humans were treated like that, how sick would we become? It is the same. Humans and animals are equally sentient beings and equally have flesh and blood but because one of them cannot speak and one has less control, it has these kinds of problems given to it.

Then, when the animals have reached one year of age, they are tied around the neck, and driven to market. The sheep are put in pens, loaded up with salt the weight of their bodies, then driven to market. They are weighed down by the salt. When they arrive they are put in pens. Some have open sores on their backs. Some have ropes tied around their shoulders and hobbles tied around their knees. Not knowing how to walk like this, they move unsteadily, jerking back and forth. Their owners without an ounce of compassion ridicule them, calling them "beasts who have no capacity for work." When they have been fed a little bad grass which does not fill their stomachs, they are left to sleep with the sharp pangs of hunger, and pains of their excessive labours. Then again, they are driven on not across one or perhaps two vast plains before stopping, but are driven on throughout the four seasons, in a non-stop experience suffering. When they get old, the words come, "This one is ready to eat", and even though that animal is not sick at all, it is led to one side away from the others, thrown to the ground on its back and there is a great commotion as it is held down while trying to escape. Its mouth is bound and it is suffocated till it dies. Others have a knife driven directly into the heart. Others have their chests cut open with a knife, and with their legs bound to their bodies, their hearts are ripped out. Good grief! How much compassion I have for the way they have to die.

They have so many sicknesses. Some of them, when they are old are declared, "ready to be sold", and are sold off in neighbouring countries such as Nepal and Bhutan. They are weighed down with very heavy loads and driven on through passes, rivers, and dangerous places to their destination. At first, they are fresh but after fifteen or twenty days have passed, their feet are destroyed by huge bloody blisters and they are murdered on the spot. They have much greater suffering than a human has when dying.

It does not go on like this for one or two lives but, as the Buddha said, animals usually have to take five or more births in a row as an animal. Sympathy, anxiousness, and more; there is no way to describe how I feel about the sufferings of these mothers of mine!

At first, when I did not understand how to eat, my parents taught me to eat. When I did not understand how to walk, they taught me to walk. When I did not understand how to speak, they taught me to speak. All of the things I did not know—arts, arithmetic, reading and writing, and so on—were taught to me by them so that I could become like other humans and enter human society. These kind fathers and mothers now have this sort of bad body, how I feel compassion for them! How awful for them!

As before, say the refuge "Guru, Three Jewels ..." Make intense supplications like before but using, "Please release them from the sufferings of the animals ..."

7. Meditation on those who have human sufferings

"Human migrators have in common the sufferings of old age, sickness, and death and have their own, individual sufferings of being blind, crippled, destitute, poor, without food, without clothing, having taxes or debts that they cannot pay, no voice to be heard, no personal power, put down by others, losing their possessions to thieves, being punished by law, separated from close ones and relatives, and so on. Thinking carefully about this, and remembering that all of these beings are none other than my kind fathers and mothers, how much compassion I have for them in misery with these sufferings." With thoughts like that, do the refuge and supplication to the guru and Jewels and dedicate the virtue as before.

Overall, think, "How would it be if I were the one experiencing the sufferings of the three bad states?", and meditate on what it would be like if it were happening to you. As Palge Rinpoche said, "That could happen very easily!" Thus, the next thing we have been instructed to contemplate is the cause of these sufferings, evil deeds.

8. Meditation on those who have done evil deeds

Generally speaking, no matter how greatly humans suffer, their suffering is not even a fraction of the suffering experienced in the bad destinies. Nonetheless, humans mostly accumulate evil deeds and go to the bad states when they die. Seeing this, one has to feel extreme compassion! Those who have been our fathers and mothers in previous lives and been immeasurably kind at the time are now the animals belonging to us. The responsibility for our food, clothing, payment of taxes and debts, and so on falls on their backs so, even in their animal births, they are kind to us like our present father and mother. Because of this, they are called, "The ones who were kind of old", and because this kindness is to be repaid, they must be singled out for care with loving kindness.

When they get old, it is declared, "They are ready to be eaten, ready to be killed" and their legs are tied up to their bodies and they are killed in various ways, such as by having their throats slit. You cannot stand it if you are just pricked by a thorn, but you don't have a whisker of concern when you kill these domestic animals who are like your kind father and mother; you treat them without the slightest care, as though they were dirt and rocks, without even a twinge of pain that feels that this is a sentient being. It has been taught that the ones who command the killing, the ones who actually do it, and the ones who eat the meat from it all have a similar level of evil deed.

Some say, "I can eat whatever food I want!" This is the talk of people whose only interest is fresh meat and the enjoyment that comes from eating it. These people enjoy the meat all the more as they chew into it, making smacking sounds while they eat, even though the meat comes from the cold-blooded killing of domestic animals who are in fact equal in kindness to their kind father and mother. But especially, regardless of which life it was in that these beings were a kind father and mother to us, these people only kill them and sell them to others when the animals have become old and have many sufferings because of it. It just makes you weep to think about it. It makes me very sad to come across people like this who can so easily reject the repayment of others' kindness.

Some people have wealth all around them but because of wanting more and more, urge others to do these things for them. As they do this, they accumulate even more evil deeds for themselves that they did not even need to make. And on top of that, they praise their helpers who they like so much for doing these kinds of evil acts. It is said that both of them are equal in their accumulation of evil deeds.

Then, there are some who steal by thievery, some who hunt, and some who are armed robbers. Some of them have had the fortune, through the kindness of the Buddha's teaching, to receive the layman's vows, bodhisatva vows, empowerments, and so on, yet they do not protect their vows. Some who wear the yellow robes disregard their vows and steal, have sexual contact, kill, practise fraud, cause conflict, do as they please even when for their own good another person tells them to stop, cause blame to be placed on others, and so on. My goodness, how awful this is; when they have drawn their last breath they will have to be born in the lower destinies. How I feel compassion for them!

It really is sad. Humans for the most part only engage in many evil deeds. They kill, sterilize animals, steal from others, engage in wrong sexuality, go back on their word, lie, denigrate other people and the dharma with bad words, gossip, engage in legal disputes, covet others belongings, have harmful thoughts, and develop wrong views. They make all sorts of evil actions based on their anger, jealousy, desire, pride, greed, deceit, and so on, and so reduce this human life to tatters without any regret. Not only that but they delight in doing as much of this wickedness as they can then showing off about it. They even teach others how to do these evil deeds while worrying that the others will change their minds and become more interested in doing good! Oh my!

The Buddha said that even each small evil deed of gossiping causes the bad destinies to be experienced for a long time[118]. He mentioned the following and others as well. Every time you bitch at someone, you have to have five hundred lives as a female dog. By barking like a dog, you will have five hundred lives as a dog. If you sit on an offering like a monkey, then you will have five hundred lives as a monkey. If you call members of the ordained sangha bad names like "shark" or "fish head", and so on, you will suffer tens of thousands of years in a body with eighteen different fish heads like shark, fish, and so on[119]. One false word uttered to another to benefit yourself to the detriment of the other will bring a long period of suffering in

---

[118] The various other elements of his exposition in this and the next paragraph are drawn from explanations about karmic cause and effect which were given by the Buddha and recorded in the sutras.

[119] Here, he is speaking of a situation in which an angry person shouted out at some monks that they were eighteen-headed sea monsters. When the person died, the Buddha explained that he had been born as an eighteen-headed sea monster because of the karma of speaking in anger to his virtuous monks.

the bad destinies and following that there will be five hundred human births in a body always without eyes, or ears, or tongue, and so on. Spitting or blowing out snot in an assembly place of the sangha brings birth in hell and killing one being has the fully-ripened result of birth in the Reviving Hell for a long period of suffering followed by three hundred to nine hundred births according to the weight of the karma. Drinking liquor results in birth in the hells for a long period where bubbling molten iron is poured into the mouth, and following that, five hundred lives as a Gyalgong[120], or yaksha[121], or madman. Wanting to eat flesh then killing animals or causing them to be killed and eating that flesh results in falling into hell for ten million millennia then having to be born as a flesh-eating bird or wild beast.

The Buddha said that, for beings who only do non-virtue, their bad actions result in not being able to have the body of a god or human for hundreds of millions of millennia and not even being able to hear of such a thing during that time. When I think about it, I have compassion for them; what they want is happiness but by their actions there will be no happiness in their future lives—isn't that so? They retract from making virtue because of seeing it as burdensome. Not one of them wants suffering but in practise, while they have the concern of not wanting the sufferings of the bad states in future lives, they only increase the extent of the evil deeds that will bring the opposite. If you think about, they are like madmen. You could call them brainless.

---

[120] A bad type of spirit.

[121] A malevolent spirit.

In regard to dharma, there are some who do not recite the mani even a little. In terms of their ability to do evil deeds, they are more expert than animals, and in fact are even worse than non-thinking animals. How I feel compassion for them!

A vicious old dog who people are afraid of going close to for fear of being bitten even when he is asleep doesn't have a single concern in his present life for the potential fearsome sufferings of the bad states in future lives. He goes about each day quite happily accumulating the karmas of the three bad destinies.

I feel sadder than sad. All of them are and have only been my kind fathers and mothers again and again. With a human body, I can understand the difference between virtue and evil—regardless of being a man or woman, rich or poor, and so on. So, now that I have at last obtained a human life, it is the right time to take the trouble to make some virtue and help myself. I have real concern for those whose mind is opposite to this and make only evil deeds for themselves; they diligently work at ensuring that they will not escape birth in the bad states. How awful is their situation! Understanding this, take refuge and make these and other supplications from your heart. "Guru, Three Jewels, and yidam deity the Great Compassionate One, look here! Please bless these beings so that they regret evil deeds and their minds turn to dharma. Please ensure that the full extent of the virtue I have created ripens on them and by doing so that their minds turn to dharma and that the doors to birth in the bad states are closed for them." Together with that, over and over arouse regret for evil deeds you have already committed, lay them aside, and retake your vows.

It is said that at this point, besides doing this sort of contemplation for the meditation on compassion, you should put aside thinking about the faults of others and think only about your own faults in this way.

Finally, even if you are not able to increase your compassion by the above means, then at least you will be able to leave aside evil deeds as though they were poison through fear of the suffering of the bad destinies that I described earlier.

Men and women householders who are not able to abandon the evil deeds connected with the consumption of meat, and other similar things, should especially meditate on compassion for animals and, having shied away from evil deeds, should do the mani, the one hundred letters with laying aside of downfalls, and the seven healers[122]. Be diligent at doing laying aside through recitation of the bodhisatva's names and make prayers of aspiration from your heart to be able to abandon these things totally. If you do that, karmas that must ripen immediately will have a smaller full-ripened effect and in the next or later lives you will be able to abandon them. And especially, when you are providing sustenance of grass and water to animals, if deaths due to famine, wild beasts, and so on occur, do not think of abandoning your activities but think, "In order to repay the kindness of these kind ones, I must continue to give them sustenance" and arouse loving kindness. Doing that is a good method for reducing the problems of this kind of full-ripening of karma.

---

[122] The should do the mani mantra of Avalokitshvara to rouse compassionate assistance for all beings, the one hundred letter mantra of Vajrasatva together with laying aside karmic downfalls in order to purify evil deeds, and the meditation of the seven healing or medicine buddhas for the general health and well-being of all.

It is a fact that men and women householders have impure motivations because of desire and that they face many difficulties of livelihood. You householders might stop eating meat and the killing involved but you are still left with the fact that all of your other food and clothing needs are fulfilled only by inflicting various types of harm and difficulty on animals. If you set aside working at your livelihood needs for a day and instead work hard at laying aside, dedication, and aspiration, that will not be able to make you happy. And then there are some who might think, "If deeds connected with flesh are that big a problem, then what about getting many gurus to stay and make offerings and worship?" The answer is that they would be doing their offerings and worship based on desire for food, so how could there be offering and worship? This is just affliction! Gurus who have the assurance of realization would want to bring those animals along and do the offering and worship together with them! We have to think, "How many of us have that kind of realization of wanting to bring them along like that?!"

To continue, since we have familiarized ourselves strongly with these bad patterns of behaviour, it is difficult for us to arouse loving kindness and compassion for the beings who harm us and harm the people we associate with. For that, it is said, we need especially to meditate on compassion. Therefore, there is the next instruction.

9. Meditation on those who cause harm

"Those who cause harm to me now have been my fathers and mothers in previous lives. Without consideration for evil deeds and suffering, bad talk, and so on, they only did things for my welfare then and because of it have experienced uncountable sufferings in the bad destinies since then. At present, the mother and son relationship is not recognized by any of us because we have migrated to other lives. At present, my own ignorance and bad karma created because of it has resulted in these fathers and mothers of previous lives harming me. I and the people who side with me see them as enemies and treat them with hostility. For their part, they abuse me, verbally twist things, steal from me, beat or hit me, and so on, and because of it they once again create the cause of having to go to the bad destinies; I have compassion for them! Each one has been my father and mother who, without consideration for evil deeds and future suffering, cared for my welfare and now they will suffer for it. Each one, pushed on by my bad karma, has harmed me and now will suffer for it. They will not be released from this suffering, suffering which comes about in dependence on me, for a long time. I am saddened by this. How much compassion I feel for them!" Think this way from deep down.

And, "These ones who have been my mother and father have helped me inestimably; how kind they are! I will arouse the enlightenment mind and then, because of wanting to accomplish buddhahood, must fully complete the six paramitas. The three paramitas of generosity, discipline, and patience are completed in dependence on sentient beings. The object of generosity is readily available: the beggars, the poor, and so on. The object of observing discipline is also readily available: it is not one person in particular but men and women as a whole, others' possessions, insects and other living beings, and so on. The object of patience is those beings who are harmful. They are very rare because there are very few beings who will harm another unless another being harms them first. Thus, I am thankful for those who harm me, because they provide me with the cause of being able to practise patience. Through them, I am able to practise patience and so complete a massive accumulation of merit; how I must thank them! Through me they create harmful acts whose full-ripening effect causes them to be born in the bad destinies; how I must have compassion for them!"

Do the refuge and supplications and prayers of aspiration from your heart like this, "Guru, Three Jewels, and yidam Avaloki-teshvara, look here! Through this may the evil deeds of harmful ones be purified! Please ensure that the full extent of the virtue I have created ripens on the harmful ones and by doing so that they are released from the sufferings of cyclic existence and the bad destinies."

It is easy to give rise to the first of those. Therefore, meditate on the kindness of mothers, and so on; it will act as a rope that will draw you on towards compassion. In the end, you need to produce a compassion that makes no distinction between enemy and friend. If you do not do that, you might produce compassion for those you find agreeable but not for those harmful ones whom you find disagreeable. However, that would be to cling in attachment to those who are friends and to be averse to those who are enemies. This approach has with it attachment and aversion which are the basis for wandering in cyclic existence and must be abandoned.

Worldly friends and enemies are nothing but impermanent; in subsequent lives there will be close friends you cannot bear to be parted from who in earlier lives were enemies that you could not stand to see and vice versa. What you see around you now in terms of friends and enemies is not fixed; except for a few beings with whom you keep pure samaya and make pure aspirations, all others will change positions when you or they pass on to another life and friends and enemies will be juggled around.

But put aside the fact that enemies and friends change around; all sentient beings have been your fathers and mothers who have been equally kind in one life or another. For some of them, you can think of repaying their kindness and for some you cannot. For those whom you cannot think of repaying their kindness, if you really give up on them, then you should be even more depressed considering the plight of those old mothers that you have now rejected. Ask yourself about this apparent real lack of embarrassment and shame. If you have a mind which really doesn't care about them, given that this mind renders you incapable of assisting your actual father and mother of this life, let alone any of the other mother and father sentient beings, it is an exceptionally important key point to habituate yourself to the unbiased thought that holds every sentient being neither close nor distant. Because of this, many holy beings, in accordance with the steps of meditation taught by the Buddha, have their own system of meditating on equanimity as a preliminary. Here, I am following the approach of Jowo Je and Unequalled Dvagpo. In their system, instead of returning the harm, whatever it might be, that mother sentient beings inflict on you, you make the commitment, "I will think only to assist them in whatever way I can and to the best of my ability."

With all of that in hand, if you continually do the refuge and supplications, "Guru, Jewels, look here!", and so on, then, through familiarization, the force of the intention involved will become greater and greater until finally, when it is fully manifest, you will become a place of refuge of all migrators, a being called a "bodhisatva".

10. Meditation on all sentient beings

Generally, all the sentient beings who pervade space are themselves pervaded by the three things afflictions, karma, and suffering. All of these sentient beings who are suffering are not just sentient beings of old but are none other than our kind fathers and mothers. None have been more or less kind than the other. None have been more or less helpful than another. Now, for the ones suffering in the hot and cold hells, I feel sympathy; for the ones suffering the pretas' hunger and thirst, I feel anxiety; for the ones suffering the animals' dumbness and stupidity, I feel gloom; for the ones suffering the asuras' fighting and strife, I feel sad; for the ones suffering the humans' evil ways, I cry; for the ones suffering the gods' transference and fall at death, I am depressed.

Overall, in the three bad destinies, beings mainly live in actual suffering; it is unbearable as described before. In the three higher levels, beings mainly live producing the causes of suffering, evil deeds. The ones in the higher levels have their eyes of intelligence blinded by the cataracts of ignorance. They have no good spiritual friend to act as their guide for the blind. Their blind-man's stick of merit has been discarded. They wander the plains of cyclic existence. They have no direction in their wandering. They are weighed down by the burden of evil deeds. They are burned by the heat of the suffering. They are pained by the thirst of the afflictions. They have neither refuge nor protector. They have many fears and harms. At death, they usually fall over the precipice of the higher levels down into the bad destinies like hailstones falling into a lake. How I feel compassion for them! How awful! I have no ability to help them and even the powerful worldly beings with their miraculous methods have no ability to help them!

Take refuge and do these supplications from your heart, "Guru, Three Jewels, and yidam Great Compassionate One, look here! Protect these sufferers, these mothers of mine! Look over them! Please make sure that all of my virtue of the three times goes to the sufferers, my fathers and mothers! Please release them from the sufferings of cyclic existence and the bad states."

And then there is this to think, too. "Who has the ability to help them? Buddha does! Therefore, if I were to become a buddha, that would be accomplished! The present buddhas themselves previously were exactly like ourselves, each of them suffering in cyclic existence. However, they aroused the enlightenment mind then, by practising and accomplishing buddhahood, became accomplished exactly like the other buddhas. Therefore, in order to benefit all of the motherly sentient beings, I have no choice but to engage in practise in order to attain buddhahood. In this world, as a human I was given two hands and as an animal however many legs; until I can repay that gift I will not rest satisfied."

There is nothing that the motherly sentient beings have not done for us. It is said that if the clothes and jewellery I have worn were gathered up into one pile, it would be larger than Mt. Sumeru. When you direct your mind to your own happiness in this and future lives, you are considering only yourself. The consideration of other types of parents is clearly visible; let alone human parents, we can see how the parents of animals care for their offspring. Without any further thought, if I see this at this time when I have obtained a body, met a guru and the holy dharma, know the advantages and disadvantages of virtue and evil and how to adopt and reject them, and do not make an effort to repay their kindness, well, who could stay unembarrassed about such selfish behaviour, who could stay unashamed at this show of non-gratitude?

At this time, you must, in order to benefit the motherly sentient beings, approach the accomplishment of buddhahood in earnest. To do that[123], firstly you must arouse the enlightenment mind then abandon evil deeds like poison. Doing so is called, "taking up the discipline of vows to prevent bad conduct". If you do evil, you put aside all ideas of being helpful to sentient beings and create the cause of having to experience the sufferings of the bad states yourself, sufferings that make you anxious just on hearing about them. There is nothing exemplary about evil deeds. Secondly, you must accomplish virtue without complacency, not thinking that your current capacity for virtue is sufficient. Doing so is called "the discipline of gathering virtuous dharmas". Thirdly, you must dedicate whatever good works you undertake and all virtue that you produce for the sake of sentient beings. Doing so is called "the discipline of working for the benefit of sentient beings".

Make the deep mental commitment, "The Buddha has said that, if I exert myself at practising the three disciplines[124] without separating from the enlightenment mind, buddhahood will be attained. Thus I will exert myself as much as I can." And, in order to have the ability to exert yourself that way, take refuge and make supplications as before starting with "Guru and the

---

[123] In this paragraph he sets out the discipline needed in relation to karmic cause and effect from the perspective of a person practising the bodhisatva's path. The three items mentioned constitute the paramita of disciple of a bodhisatva.

[124] ... of the paramita of a bodhisatva ...

Three Jewels, look here!" In addition to that, practise them to the extent you are capable and think again and again on the eight thoughts of great beings.

If you have produced a little compassion, then there are the two, wondrous, secret paths of the conquerors' sons which are unheard of amongst the noble shravakas and noble pratyekabuddhas even in their dreams—what need to mention all other migrators—for you to learn. It is very important to look for gurus who can teach you about them and request the teaching.[125]

The system of meditation on compassion that references sentient beings shown here[126] is based on the understanding of many holy masters presented in such texts as: the *Kadampa Volumes of Scripture* and others which are the excellent speech of Jowo Je and his lineage holders; Unequalled Dvagpo's *Stages of the Path*[127]; a revealed treasure of Guru Rinpoche which is an

---

[125] He is referring to the development of the two types of enlightenment mind, fiction and superior fact. See the glossary for them.

[126] There are three compassions mentioned at the beginning of Chandrakirti's *Entrance to the Middle Way* which is what he is referring to here: compassion referencing sentient beings, compassion referencing the dharma, and non-referencing compassion. They are presented in order of profundity. Moreover, the first two are fictional enlightenment mind, the last is superior fact enlightenment mind. Here, his discussion has been about compassion referencing—developed in view of—the situation of sentient beings.

[127] Gampopa wrote several texts in the Kadampa Stages of the Path

(continued ...)

instruction manual on Guhyasamaja; the great hearing lineage of the talks of the conquerors' son Thogmey Zangpo; Jetsun Taranatha's *Stages of the Path*; Kongtrul Rinpoche's *Mind Training*; and others. I have used the vernacular subject which is a little less hard to understand so that those of lesser intelligence could easily understand.

3. RELATED MATTERS THAT FOLLOW

If the compassion that references sentient beings is properly produced first, the two subsequent compassions will naturally be produced at the same time. Therefore I see that it is very important for us beginners, ordinary lay people, to be assiduous at the first one.

Train in the compassion that references sentient beings for seven days at least, then months or years, whatever you can. Then, if you keep doing it as a regular practice, do it by doing the ones before and after the fourth and this will include the fourth. If you find it hard to understand because of having a weaker intellect, then meditate both on the second point about mothers and on the ninth point about harmful beings and if you train based on what you understand from emphasizing each of these, then that will summarize and include all of the meaning.

In general, when there is some faith in dharma, whether there is a higher level of intelligence or not, it is true for everyone—man or woman, high or low in society, shepherd or master or servant—that listening over and over to the dharma read out

---

[127] (... continued)
style.

aloud by someone who can read well, does help the mindstream a little. It is a key point to connect with the instructions on compassion found in the life stories of the conquerors' sons, the *Bodhisatva Stages*[128], and the Dzogchen text, *The Words of My Excellent Teacher*[129].

When there is no faith, it is said there is nothing even the Buddha, let alone others, can do. And then, for someone like myself with a mind that resists dharma, it is really difficult to do anything that could help. You might have heard a lot of dharma but it is possible that you might refuse to listen to it and find that it turns into not being helpful. And, after that, no matter what you hear, you just pass it off, thinking, "Oh yes, it is talked about like that", and then as it is said, you find that it has become impossible to digest and understand it. So there is the saying, "Toughness can be overcome with oil but not if the oil is butter inside its packing!" Accordingly, it is said that people with evil deeds can be tamed by dharma but not if they are resistant to it.

Even if that does not apply to you, whether you are intelligent or not, it is important to push yourself. It is said that if you think about yourself, "This corpse of a person cannot understand" and you lose your drive and just sit there in self-defeat when you cannot understand the dharma, then you will never be able to understand it throughout the course of all your lives and will never be released from suffering. Even if you are a

---

[128] A text of Asanga that details the boshisatva journey.

[129] A text by Dzogchen Patrul that contains extensive explanations of the preliminary practices, common and uncommon, for vajra vehicle practice.

person who does not understand anything at all, if you do not sit in self-defeat but push yourself and listen and listen and ask and ask, then even in this life you will gain a partial understanding and in later lives will understand without difficulty and thus will gradually release yourself from suffering. I see this as a key point which is very important for people in the lower classes of society to understand.

It is quite possible to give rise to the highest level of compassion even without having a great understanding of all that can be explained. People with the lowest understanding can fear the sufferings of the bad states then intently practise virtue and avoid evil and if they do, it will benefit their minds. However, if they are not intent on it, even if they memorize the words, it will not benefit their minds. Furthermore, this is the root of the sutras and tantras so please do understand that yes, getting the scriptural transmission is important but, even if you do not get it, the actual practice of it is something that all men and women who have faith and devotion can and should do[130]. In the case of mantra, it is necessary to have the scriptural transmission. However, and as Chagmey Rinpoche[131] pointed out, in the case of sutra, even if you do not obtain the scriptural transmission, it is correct to do the practice.

There is great benefit to staying in retreat meditating on compassion and reciting the mani mantra of Avalokiteshvara. It is much better than meditating on development stage when that

---

[130] Here he is criticising the very bad Tibetan habit of running to get empowerments and scriptural reading transmissions but never practising what has been obtained.

[131] Chagmey Rinpoche was a great Kagyu master.

meditation is done without knowledge of logic, reference, and realisation and done with concrete fixation on a self. Avalokiteshvara is known as the Great Compassionate One but the real Avalokiteshvara is great compassion without reference[132]. If you do not have compassion but recite the mani mantra, it is said that it is not the mantra of Avalokiteshvara, so compassion is an extremely important point in that practice.

But more than that, if you do not have compassion, then no matter what dharma you practise, it does not become part of the practice of the Great Vehicle and, because of that, it is not possible to attain buddhahood by doing it. If you have compassion, all of the dharmas taught by the Buddha are gathered up, just as when you call out to guests to come. As Unequalled Dvagpo said,

> If you do not train your mind in the method, great compassion, the path sinks to being one of the Lesser Vehicle.

And in *Inexhaustible Intellect's Sutra* it says,

> For example, just as the movement in and out of breath is the preliminary to the life faculty of humans, likewise, the great compassion of the bodhisattva is the preliminary for the true accomplishment of the Great Vehicle.

And, the *Vairochana Sambodhi* says,

---

[132] Without reference means without dualistic mind. He is saying that compassion is not the conceptual idea of it that so many Buddhists have but compassion which is integral to wisdom.

> The Owner of the Secret's[133] wisdom that knows everything comes from the root, compassion ...

And, the *Sutra that Authentically Sums Up Dharma* says,

> The bhagavat and bodhisatvas hold firmly to one dharma and, having realised it fully, all the dharmas of a buddha are in the palm of the hand. What is this one dharma? It is this: great compassion. Oh Bhagavat, with great compassion, all of the dharmas of a buddha are in the palms of the bodhisatva's hands. Oh Bhagavat, if I make an example of it, wherever the precious wheel of a chakravartin emperor goes, all the hosts of troops go. Oh Bhagavat, likewise, whenever the great compassion of the bodhisatvas goes, all the dharmas of a buddha go. Oh Bhagavat, if I make an example of it, if the life faculty goes, the other faculties also will go. Oh Bhagavat, likewise, if the great compassion goes, all the dharmas of a bodhisatva also will arise.

Buddhahood is obtained and then, after that, the power of compassion cares for the migrators equal to space. In regard to this, when the *Fifty Verses of Praise* says "these migrators ..." it means that the immeasurable welfare of beings performed by a buddha for "these migrators" arises from compassion. For that reason, the *Entrance to the Middle Way* says, "To start with, I must prostrate to the Buddha and must prostrate to compassion" and then goes on to explain the meaning of compassion with "whatever love is ..." Chagmed Rinpoche explains the meaning behind the words "To start with I must prostrate to compassion" as follows like this:

---

[133] Vajrapani.

First, when buddhahood is to be obtained,
It is like a seed, it is said.
In the middle, the conditions for obtaining
    buddhahood
Are explained as the manure and water when
    farming.
Finally, when buddhahood has been obtained,
Enlightened activity, the one door to the welfare of
    migrators,
Is like a perfect harvest.
It arises from compassion, the Buddha taught.
Shravaka and pratyekabuddhas arhats, and so on,
Arise from the teachings of the Bhagavat;
All of the complete buddhas, the bhagavats,
Are born from the bodhisatvas;
All of the bodhisattvas in turn
Are born from compassion because of which
The root of dharma is compassion.

Orgyan Rinpoche[134] said,

If there is no compassion, the root of dharma is
    ruined.

And Jetsun Milarepa said,

As a consequence of meditating and meditating on
    loving kindness and compassion,
We remember to cherish others.
If we do not meditate on cherishing others more than
    ourselves,
How can our nice words of compassion be of benefit?

---

[134] Padmasambhava.

And Dromton Rinpoche said,

> He[135] asked one practitioner what Putowa, Phuchungwa, Gonpawa, and Khamlungpa were doing. The practitioner replied, 'Putowa is teaching dharma to many hundreds of sangha'. 'There is one thing even more amazing than that', came the reply. 'Phuchungwa is erecting many representations of body, speech, and mind'. 'There is one thing even more amazing than that', came the reply. 'Gonpawa just stays put doing nothing but meditation'. 'There is one thing even more amazing than that', came the reply. Khamlungpa is at Drogpo Mountain; he sits there with his head covered over, crying. Rinpoche took off his hat, pressed his hands together at his heart, wept, and said, 'That is extremely amazing. Doing dharma? He is the one who is doing dharma! He has many qualities to speak of but if I tell them to you, he would not be pleased'.

Langtang Rinpoche prostrated to Chen Ngawa and said, "From today onwards I would like to meditate on loving kindness and compassion." Chen Ngawa removed his hat, put his hands together at his heart and said three times, "Truly excellent!"

If authentic compassion is meditated on: because the Buddha and his sons think of you as their child and family member, it is the supreme refuge; because it pleases all the buddhas, it is the supreme offering; because it benefits all sentient beings, it is the supreme gift; because it purifies immeasurable evil deeds, it is

---

[135] Atisha asked one person who came along about Atisha's own, principal students.

the supreme laying aside; because it becomes the best place of offering for all migrators, it is the supreme purifier of mishandled faith offerings; because it leads to birth in the fields of the buddhas, it is the supreme transference; because unfathomable merit arises from it, it is the supreme accumulation of merit; because, if compassion is taken up, the deeds of the world for the most part become the cause of attaining enlightenment, it is the supreme oral instruction; and because buddhahood is quickly obtained through it, it is the supreme of profound dharmas.

In short, the root of every possible happiness and good thing in the fields of samsara and nirvana is met with in compassion for the reason that, if there is no compassion, buddhahood does not occur, and if buddhahood does not occur, the rest does not occur. Following on from that, the very essence of the eighty-four thousand dharmas is the two things of emptiness and compassion. Emptiness is the general path of the four types of noble ones and the root of fictional enlightenment mind, compassion, is the path only for the conquerors' sons who practise to become a buddha. A more complete description of the benefits of enlightenment mind can be found in the *Gandavyuha Sutra* where about two hundred and thirty examples are given; and it is taught extensively in *Entering the Bodhisatva's Conduct*, and others like it; and, it is also taught in the *Translated Word* and *Translated Treatises*[136]—so please see those to learn more.

Fictional enlightenment mind is like the father of the family line that gives birth to a buddha. The foregoing has explained

---

[136] *Translated Word* is the Tibetan Kangyur and *Translated Treatises* the Tibetan Tangyur.

a little about compassion which is the root of fictional enlightenment mind and about the techniques of the meditation on it and benefits of it.

The ultimate, superior fact enlightenment mind is like the mother of the family line that gives birth to a buddha. It is the root of all dharmas. Now I will explain a little about it.

Gyalsay Rinpoche said,

> However it appears, this is one's own mind.
> Mindness is free from all extremes of elaboration
> from the outset.
> When that is cognized, all the conceptual labels of
> grasped and grasper[137]
> Are no longer done in mind[138]; that is the practice of
> the conqueror's sons.

---

[137] Samsaric mind, from a Mind Only or tantric perspective, makes the mistake of a dualistic split. The one awareness comes to believe that, on this side so to speak, there is the *grasper* or apprehender which is the knowing mind, and that on the other side so to speak, there are the objects of the senses that are *grasped* at or apprehended by the grasper. This kind of dualistic mind does not know the objects of consciousness in direct perception but only through referencing *conceptual* bits of stuff which are *labels* of that actual experience.

[138] When that process is seen through and the various elaborations that constitute samsaric mind are seen through and eliminated, one returns to the innate fact of one's own mind, which is entirely freed at that point of the dualized grasped and grasper. That is the superior fact enlightenment mind practice of the bodhisatvas.

The first two lines of the verses are the view, the latter two lines are the way to meditate on it, and that overall is the way of going about the accomplishment of buddhahood.

In that verse it says, "… are no longer done in mind." These are the key words of Hvashang whose view has been vigorously refuted but the meaning here is different[139]. These words, according to the way it is set out in the Kagyu system of the All-Knowing, Unequalled Dvagpo Rinpoche, mean this: motivated by great compassion, you remain self-settled with no distraction, no meditation, and no alteration and allow the liveliness to come forth within devotion[140]. Just as my supreme guide and chief refuge Chowang Rinpoche said,

> The ground view is the inseparability of samsara and
>   nirvana;
> The path meditation is no alteration, without
>   grasping;
> The life energy of conduct is compassion pervasive as
>   space.

The lineage holders of the Old Translations system have the same approach as that. Or, if you prefer the great being Lord Tsongkhapa's approach, as he says,

---

[139] The words are a specific Tibetan term "yid la mi byed pa". Hvashang used them to mean that one simply stops thinking with the mentality of dualistic mind. The meaning referred to here, and the correct one, is that the whole process of involvement with that dualistic mind is seen through and eliminated in the process.

[140] These are Vajra Vehicle instructions on how to do this kind of practice.

> First seek out certainty of the view in which both
> emptiness and appearance are present without either
> emptiness or dependent relationship being
> contradicted. Then meditate in analytical and resting
> modes in a state which is apprehending lack of
> nature.

At any rate, no matter what kind of instruction you have received—Madhyamaka, Mahamudra, or Maha Ati—since the best result is to attain realization, middling is to gain experience, and worst is only to have an intellectual understanding, it is crucial to work at the instructions assiduously and with very great effort. After all, the goal you are aiming for might be something of immeasurable benefits but you have to realize the goal in order to get those benefits.

These two types of precious enlightenment mind are the very heart of all of the sutras, tantras, and inner oral instructions. The innumerable dharma doors contained within the two things of accumulation and purification can only be brought about in one way: the two types of enlightenment mind must first be produced, then unified, and then developed further and further until they been trained up to total completion—which is called "true complete buddhahood".

Compassion is the root of the two enlightenment minds and
    of the Great Vehicle;
I have no experience of its meditation so have written
This clear summary of the method of its meditation
    according to the intent of the holy ones
In words that are not elegant but are easy to understand,
Without going to a lot of trouble, just for the benefit of my
    own mind.

This might not be helpful but at least it is not tainted by ideas
     of fame and gain,
Therefore the guardians should not be worried, I think.
Nonetheless, because I do not have a sesame-seed's worth of
     the good qualities
Needed to make this beneficial to the teaching and migrators,
If there is something mistaken here, I lay it aside in front of
The embodiment of the supreme refuges, and ask them to
     correct it.

It is offered to the faithful and virtuous ones here in
     Chogdrong district:
May this clear exposition of the ways of virtue assist
All those men and women who do mani retreats.
If you do not listen to what I have said because of finding it
     not to be useful,
Then I have nothing else that could be of help.

I have karma, afflictions, and all of the fetters because of
     which
I am not certain about where I will go in the next life.
And, leaving aside the ability to help others,
Apart from what you have actually met with here,
I have nothing else to say that could be of benefit.

I have written these words in the vernacular but
The meaning here is the excellent path of the Great Vehicle,
Therefore I think that, if you practise it, it can help.
For persons of middling faculties on up it should
Be plain as day what to do with these instructions
But for persons of the least faculties—ones like myself of
     inferior intelligence

Who have some kind of virtuous mind even if they are poor
    at developing it further,
The ones who seem unable to follow a holy master,
I tell you that seeing this is like discovering a treasure in the
    palm of your hand and say to you
"Please practise it with great joy and delight!"

By the virtue of writing this may I and all these people related
    to
The motherly migrators equal to space,
Men and women alike become bodhisatvas, then
Accomplish the supreme noble one, Avalokiteshvara,
And become buddhas in the field of Sukhavati.

It is a long time now since a Buddhist layman who devotes himself to the practice of the enlightenment mind and who has the jewel ornaments of the noble ones, someone who I hold as a dear friend, came asking me to write down the way to do each of the meditations of guru yoga and so on. And my dharma friend, the full monk Tobla, also has asked me again and again to help him by writing a little about the key points of meditation. And then there are many people of the Chogdrong district, virtuous minded men and women who stay in retreat reciting the mani, whom I thought to help. Primarily though, because of my own interest in the Great Vehicle and Avalokiteshvara and my inability to arouse the compassion which is the root of each of those two, I, Karma Ngedon Tengyay or Lion of Explanations, who is sustained below the refuge, the guru sovereign over the four types of compassion, The Holder of The Lotus, Glorious Karmapa, and his lineage, wrote this in order to jog my mind about the subject on the eighth lunar day of the month Pushya.

Glossary of Terms

Affliction, Skt. kleśha, Tib. nyon mongs: This term is usually translated as emotion or disturbing emotion, etcetera, but the Buddha was very specific about the meaning of this word. When the Buddha referred to the emotions, meaning a movement of mind, he did not refer to them as such but called them "kleśha" in Sanskrit, meaning exactly "affliction". It is a basic part of the Buddhist teaching that emotions afflict beings, giving them problems at the time and causing more problems in the future.

Alpha purity, Tib. ka dag: A Great Completion term meaning purity that is there from the first, that is, primordial purity. There are many terms in Buddhism that express the notion of "primordial purity" but this one is unique to the Great Completion teaching. The term "alpha purity" matches the Tibetan term both literally and in meaning.

Assurance, Tib. gdeng: Although often translated as confidence, this term means assurance with all of the extra meaning conveyed by that term. A bird might be confident of its ability to fly but more than that, it has the assurance that it will not fall to the ground because of knowing that it has wings and the training to use them. Similarly, a person might be confident that he could liberate the afflictions but not be assured of doing so because of lack of training or other causes. However, a person who has accumulated the causes to be able to liberate afflictions is assured of the ability to do so.

Bodhicitta: see under enlightenment mind.

Capable One, Skt. muni, Tib. thub pa: The term "muni" as for example in "Shakyamuni" has long been thought to mean "sage" because of an entry in Monier-Williams excellent Sanskrit-English dictionary. In fact, it has been used by many Indian religions since the times of ancient India to mean someone "who could withstand the rigours of gaining spiritual attainment".

Chakravartin Emperor, Skt. chakravartirāja: This refers to a king of one of four levels of sovereignty. Each king has a thousand-spoked wheel in his possession whose metal symbolizes the extent of his domain. The king of least domain has an iron wheel and rules over a whole Mt. Meru system, such as ours; the next has a copper wheel and rules over a cosmic region of one thousand Mt. Meru systems; the next has a silver wheel and rules over a cosmic region of one thousand of the thousand-fold Mt. Meru systems; and the next has a gold wheel and rules over an entire third-order thousand-fold world system. The king with a gold wheel is said to be equal to a supreme nirmanakaya buddha in terms of his domain of power but is a secular ruler rather than a religious one.

Clinging, Tib. zhen pa: In Buddhism, this term refers specifically to the twofold process of dualistic mind mis-taking things that are not true, not pure, as true, pure, etcetera and then, because of seeing them as highly desirable even though they are not, attaching itself to or clinging to those things. This type of clinging acts as a kind of glue that keeps a person joined to the unsatisfactory things of cyclic existence because of mistakenly seeing them as desirable.

Compassionate activity, Tib. thugs rje: This does not mean compassionate activity in general. Rather, it is a specific term of the most profound level of teachings of Mahāmudrā and Great Completion. These teachings describe innate wisdom as having three characteristics. The third characteristic is this compassionate activity. It refers to the fact that wisdom spontaneously does whatever needs to be done, throughout all reaches of time and space, for all beings. Although it includes the word "compassion" in its name, it is more primordial than that. It is the dynamic quality of enlightenment which choice-lessly, ceaselessly, spontaneously, and pervasively acts to benefit others. The term is often used in discussions of Great Completion and essence Mahāmudrā.

Concept label, Tib. mtshan ma: This is the technical name for the structures or concepts which function as the words of concep-tual mind's language. They are the very basis of operation of the third aggregate and hence of the way that dualistic mind communicates with its world. For example, a table seen in direct visual perception will have no concept labels involved with knowing it. However, when thought becomes involved and there is the thought "table" in an inferential or conceptual perception of the table, the name-tag "table" will be used to reference the table and that name tag is the concept label.

Although we usually reference phenomena via these concepts, the phenomena are not the dualistically referenced things we think of them as being. The actual fact of the phenomena is quite different from the concept labels used to discursively think about them and is known by wisdom rather than concept-based mind. Therefore, this term is often used in Buddhist literature to signify that dualistic samsaric mind is involved rather than non-dualistic wisdom.

Confusion, Tib. 'khrul pa: In Buddhism, this term mostly refers to the fundamental confusion of taking things the wrong way that happens because of fundamental ignorance, although it can also have the more general meaning of having lots of thoughts and being confused about it. In the first case, it is defined like this "Confusion is the appearance to rational mind of something being present when it is not" and refers, for example, to seeing an object, such as a table, as being truly present, when in fact it is present only as mere, interdependent appearance.

Cyclic existence: See under saṃsāra.

Dharmakaya, Skt. dharmakāya, Tib. chos sku: In the general teachings of Buddhism, this refers to the mind of a buddha, with "dharma" meaning reality and "kāya" meaning body. In the Thorough Cut practice of Great Completion it additionally has the special meaning of being the means by which one rapidly imposes liberation on oneself.

Elaboration, Tib. spro ba: This is a general name for what is given off by dualistic mind as it goes about its conceptual process. In general, elaborations prevent a person from seeing emptiness directly. Freedom from elaborations implies direct sight of emptiness.

Enlightenment mind, Skt. bodhicitta, Tib. byang chub sems: This is a key term of the Great Vehicle. It is the type of mind that is connected not with the lesser enlightenment of an arhat but with the enlightenment of a truly complete buddha. As such, it is a mind which is connected with the aim of bringing all sentient beings to that same level of buddhahood. A person who has engendered this mind has by definition entered the Great Vehicle and is either a bodhisatva or a buddha.

It is important to understand that "enlightenment mind" is used to refer equally to the minds of all levels of bodhisatva on the path to buddhahood and to the mind of a buddha who has completed the path. Therefore, it is not "mind striving for enlightenment" as is so often translated, but "enlightenment mind", meaning that kind of mind which is connected with the full enlightenment of a truly complete buddha and which is present in all those who belong to the Great Vehicle. The term is used in the conventional Great Vehicle and also in the Vajra Vehicle. In the Vajra Vehicle, there are some special uses of the term where substances of the pure aspect of the subtle physical body are understood to be manifestations of enlightenment mind.

Equipoise, Tib. mnyam bzhag: Equipoise is the state of evenly resting in one-pointed concentration on an object of meditation.

Evil, evil deed, Skt. papaṃ, Tib. sdig pa: The original Sanskrit means something which someone has done which is truly bad, rotten. Anyone who has done such a thing is looked down upon. The Tibetan for it relates to the idea of a scorpion, a nasty creature that will sting you and injure you. In Buddhism, the term does not have the Christian sense of evil but simply means action done that, being done under the influence of an affliction, degrades you now in other's eyes, degrades you now because of the bad karmic seeds that you have planted by doing it, and degrades you in the future because of the ripening of the bad karmas into unpleasant results.

Fictional, Skt. saṃvṛti, Tib. kun rdzob: This term is paired with the term "superior factual" *q.v.* Until now these two terms have been translated as "relative" and "absolute" but these translations are nothing like the original terms. These terms are extremely important in the Buddhist teaching so it is very important that they be corrected, but more than that, if the actual meaning of these terms is not presented, then the teaching connected with them cannot be understood.

The Sanskrit term saṃvṛti means a deliberate invention, a fiction, a hoax. It refers to the mind of ignorance which, because of being obscured and so not seeing suchness, is not true but a fiction. The things that appear to that ignorance are therefore fictional. Nonetheless, the beings who live in this ignorance believe that the things that appear to them through the filter of ignorance are true, are real. Therefore, these beings live in fictional truth.

Fictional and superior factual: Fictional and superior factual are our greatly improved translations for "relative" and "absolute" respectively. Briefly, the original Sanskrit word for fiction means a deliberately produced *fiction* and refers to the world projected by a mind controlled by ignorance as being real. The original word for superior fact means "that *superior fact* that appears on the surface of the mind of a noble one who has transcended saṃsāra" and refers to reality seen as it actually is. Relative and absolute do not convey this meaning at all and, when they are used, the meaning being presented is simply lost.

Fictional truth, Skt. saṃvṛtisatya, Tib. kun rdzob bden pa: See under fictional.

Fictional truth enlightenment mind, Tib. kun rdzob bden pa'i byang chub sems: One of a pair of terms explained in the Great Vehicle; the other is Superior Fact Truth Enlightenment Mind. See under fictional truth and superior fact truth for information about those terms. Enlightenment mind is defined as two types. The fictional type is the conventional type. It is explained as consisting of love and great compassion within the framework of an intention to obtain truly complete enlightenment for the sake of all sentient beings. The superior factual truth type is the ultimate type. It is explained as the enlightenment mind that is directly perceiving emptiness.

Field, Field realm, Tib. zhing, zhing khams: This term is often translated "buddha field" though there is no "buddha" in the term. There are many different types of "fields" in both saṃsāra and nirvāṇa. Thus there are fields that belong to enlightenment and ones that belong to ignorance. Moreover, just as there are "realms" of saṃsāra—desire, form, and formless—so there are realms of nirvāṇa—the fields dharmakāya, saṃbhogakāya, and nirmāṇakāya and these are therefore called "field realms".

Foremost instruction, Skt. upadeśha, Tib. man ngag: There are several types of instruction mentioned in Buddhist literature: there is the general level of instruction which is the meaning contained in the words of the texts of the tradition; on a more personal and direct level there is oral instruction which has been passed down from teacher to student from the time of the buddha; and on the most profound level there are foremost instructions which are not only oral instructions provided by one's guru but are special, core instructions that come out of personal experience and which convey the teaching concisely and with the full weight of personal experience.

Grasped-grasping, Tib. gzung 'dzin: When mind is turned outwardly as it is in the normal operation of dualistic mind, it has developed two faces that appear simultaneously. Special names are given to these two faces: mind appearing in the form of the external object being referenced is called "that which is grasped at" and mind appearing in the form of the consciousness that is registering it is called the "grasper" or "grasping" of it. Thus, there is the term "grasped-grasper" or "grasped-grasping" which is a convenient abbreviation for the mode of operation of dualistic mind. Moreover, when these two terms are used, it alerts one to the fact that a Mind Only style of presentation is being discussed. This pair of terms pervades Mind Only, Middle Way, and tantric writings and is exceptionally important in all of them.

Note that one could substitute the word "apprehended" for "grasped" and "apprehender" for "grasper" or "grasping" and that would reflect one connotation of the original Sanskrit terminology. The solidified duality of grasped and grasper is nothing but an invention of dualistic thought; it has that kind of character.

Great Completion, Tib. rdzogs pa chen po: Two main practices of reality developed in the Buddhist traditions of ancient India and then came to Tibet: Great Completion (Mahāsandhi) and Great Seal (Mahāmudrā). Great Completion and Great Seal are names for reality and names for a practice that directly leads to that reality. Their ways of describing reality and their practices are very similar. The Great Completion teachings are the pinnacle teachings of the tantric teachings of Buddhism that first came into Tibet with Padmasambhava and his peers and were later kept alive in the Nyingma (Earlier Ones) tradition. The Great Seal practice came into Tibet later and was held in the Sakya and Kagyu lineages. Later again, the Great Seal was held by the Gelugpa lineage, which obtained its transmissions of the instructions from the Sakya and Kagyu lineages.

It is popular nowadays to call Great Completion by the name Great Perfection, though that is a mistake. The original name Mahāsandhi refers to that one space of reality in which all things come together. Thus it means "completeness" or "completion" as the Tibetans chose to translate it and does not imply or contain the sense of "perfection".

Great Vehicle, Skt. mahāyāna, Tib. theg pa chen po: The Buddha's teachings as a whole can be summed up into three vehicles where a vehicle is defined as that which can carry a person to a certain destination. The first vehicle, called the Lesser Vehicle, contains the teachings designed to get an individual moving on the spiritual path through showing the unsatisfactory state of cyclic existence and an emancipation from that. However, that path is only concerned with personal emancipation and fails to take account of all of the beings that there are in existence. There used to be eighteen schools of Lesser

Vehicle in India but the only one surviving nowadays is the Theravāda of south-east Asia. The Greater Vehicle is a step up from that. The Buddha explained that it was great in comparison to the Lesser Vehicle for seven reasons. The first of those is that it is concerned with attaining the truly complete enlightenment of a truly complete buddha for the sake of every sentient being where the Lesser Vehicle is concerned only with a personal liberation that is not truly complete enlightenment and which is achieved only for the sake of that practitioner. The Great Vehicle has two divisions: a conventional form in which the path is taught in a logical, conventional way, and an unconventional form in which the path is taught in a very direct way. This latter vehicle is called the Vajra Vehicle because it takes the innermost, indestructible (vajra) fact of reality of one's own mind as the vehicle to enlightenment.

Guardian, Skt. nātha, Tib. mgon po: This name is a respectful title reserved for the buddhas and highly-developed bodhisatvas. It means that they both protect and nurture sentient beings who they oversee, like a child who, having no parents has been given or has found a guardian. It is often translated as "protector" but that correctly translates another Sanskrit term to start with and on top of that is insufficient because it does not include the aspect of nurturing. It is also given to other beings such as bodhisatvas who have a similar quality, for example, Guardian Nāgārjuna and Guardian Maitreya.

Kagyu, Tib. bka' brgyud: There are four main schools of Buddhism in Tibet—Nyingma, Kagyu, Sakya, and Gelug. Nyingma is the oldest school dating from about 800 C.E. Kagyu and Sakya both appeared in the 12th century C.E. Each of these three schools came directly from India. The Gelug school came later and did not come directly from India but came from the other three. The Nyingma school holds the tantric teachings called Great Completion (Dzogchen); the other three schools hold the tantric teachings called Mahāmudrā. Kagyu practitioners often join Nyingma practice with their Kagyu practice and Kagyu teachers often teach both, so it is common to hear about Kagyu and Nyingma together.

Kaya, Skt. kāya, Tib. sku: The Sanskrit term means a functional or coherent collection of parts, similar to the French "corps", and hence also comes to mean "a body". It is used in Tibetan Buddhist texts specifically to distinguish bodies belonging to the enlightened side from ones belonging to the samsaric side.

Enlightened being in Buddhism is said to be comprised of one or more kāyas. It is most commonly explained to consist of one, two, three, four, or five kāyas, though it is pointed out that there are infinite aspects to enlightened being and therefore it can also be said to consist of an infinite number of kāyas. In fact, these descriptions of enlightened being consisting of one or more kāyas are given for the sake of understanding what is beyond conceptual understanding so should not be taken as absolute statements.

Latency, Skt. vāsanā, Tib. bag chags: The original Sanskrit has the meaning exactly of "latency". The Tibetan term translates that inexactly with "something sitting there (Tib. chags) within the environment of mind (Tib. bag)". Although it has become popular to translate this term into English with "habitual pattern", that is not its meaning. The term refers to a karmic seed that has been imprinted on the mindstream and is present there as a latency, ready and waiting to come into manifestation.

Lay aside, Tib. bshags pa: This term is usually translated as "confession" but that is not the meaning. The term literally means to cut something away and remove it from oneself. In Buddhism, it is used in the context of ridding oneself of the karmic seeds sown by bad karmic actions.

Buddhism is a totally non-theistic religion, so it is very important to understand that one is not confessing wrongdoings to anyone, including oneself. There is no granting of absolution in this system. As the Buddha himself said, he has no ability to purify the karmic stains of sentient beings, he can only teach them how to do so. The practice that he taught for ridding oneself of karmic wrongdoings is the practice of realizing for oneself that they hold the seed of future suffering, rousing regret, and distancing oneself from them. In doing so, one lays them aside.

There is a longer phrase that indicates the full practice of laying aside. The Tibetan phrase "mthol zhing shags pa" literally means "admitting and laying aside". Note that "admitting" also does not entail confession; it refers to that fact that one first has to admit or acknowledge to oneself that one has done something wrong, karmically speaking, and that it will have undesirable consequences. Without this, one cannot effectively take the second step of distancing oneself from the actions. Therefore, it is explained that the process of "laying aside" has to be understood to include the practice of "admission" because, without that acknowledgement, the laying aside cannot be done.

Lesser Vehicle, Skt. hīnayāna, Tib. theg pa dman pa: See under Great Vehicle.

Lustre, Tib. mdangs: In both Mahamudra and Great Completion there is the general term "gdangs" meaning what is given off or emitted by something in general, for example the sound given off by a loudspeaker or what the empty factor of mind emits. The Mahamudra teaching makes no difference between that term and this term "mdangs" but the Great Completion teaching does. In Great Completion, this term has the more refined meaning of "lustre" or a subtle output. In this teaching, there is the output of the empty aspect of mind altogether but there is also the lustre of that emptiness.

Maha Ati, Skt. mahāti, Tib. shin tu chen po: Mahā Ati or Ati Yoga is the name of the ninth and last of the nine vehicles taught in the Nyingma system of nine vehicles. The name "ati" literally means that it is the vehicle at the end of the sequence of all other vehicles. It is not only the final vehicle at the end of the sequence but the peak of all vehicles given that it presents reality more directly than any of the vehicles below it. It is therefore also called the king of vehicles.

"Mahāsandhi"—"Dzogpa Chenpo" in the Tibetan language and "Great Completion" in the English language—is the name of the teachings on reality contained in the Maha Ati vehicle and also of the reality itself. Great Completion and Maha Ati are often used interchangeably even through their references are slightly different. See Great Completion in the glossary for more.

Mahamudra, Skt. mahāmudrā, Tib. phyag rgya chen po: Mahāmudrā is the name of a set of ultimate teachings on reality and also of the reality itself. This is explained at length in the book *Gampopa's Mahamudra: The Five-Part Mahamudra of the Kagyus* by Tony Duff, published by Padma Karpo Translation Committee, 2008, ISBN 978-9937-2-0607-5.

Mara, Skt. māra, Tib. bdud: A Sanskrit term closely related to the word "death". Buddha spoke of four classes of extremely negative influences that have the capacity to drag a sentient being deep into saṃsāra. They are the "maras" or "kiss of death": of having a samsaric set of five skandhas; of having afflictions; of death itself; and of the son of gods, which means being seduced and taken in totally by sensuality.

Migrator, Tib. 'gro ba: Migrator is one of several terms that were commonly used by the Buddha to mean "sentient being". It shows sentient beings from the perspective of their constantly being forced to go here and there from one rebirth to another by the power of karma. They are like flies caught in a jar, constantly buzzing back and forth. The term is often translated using "beings" which is another general term for sentient beings, but doing so loses the meaning entirely. Buddhist authors who know the tradition do not use the word loosely but use it specifically to give the sense of beings who are constantly and helplessly going from one birth to another, and that is how the term should be read. The term "six migrators" refers to the six types of migrators within samsaric existence—hell-beings, pretas, animals, humans, demi-gods, and gods.

Mind, Skt. chitta, Tib. sems: There are several terms for mind in the Buddhist tradition, each with its own, specific meaning. This term is the most general term for the samsaric type of mind. It refers to the type of mind that is produced because of fundamental ignorance of enlightened mind. Whereas the wisdom of enlightened mind lacks all complexity and knows in a non-dualistic way, this mind of un-enlightenment is a very complicated apparatus that only ever knows in a dualistic way.

The Mahāmudrā and Great Completion teachings use the terms "entity of mind" and "mind's entity" to refer to what this complicated, samsaric mind is at core—the enlightened form of mind.

Mindness, Skt. chittatā, Tib. sems nyid: The Sanskrit term is made up of two parts "chitta" and "tā" and the Tibetan term, following that, also is made up of two parts "sems" and "nyid". The first part in each case is straightforward, with "chitta" and "sems" both referring to "mind". The second part in each case is a grammatical term that modifies the preceding word.

Both Sanskrit and Tibetan grammars define the second part, "tā" and "nyid" respectively, as having two distinct usages. The first is that it points out something, similar in English to the pronoun "that". Thus, in the case here, the overall meaning is "samsaric mind itself, just that" or you could also say "the samsaric mind". The second is that it points out the very essence ore core of that something, similar in English to adding "-ness" to the end of a word. Thus, in the case here, the overall meaning is "the essence or core of samsaric mind, what it is at root".

The term "mindness" that conveys the second of the two distinct usages is one of many terms that indicate the essence of samsaric mind, what samsaric mind is at its very core". Thus, this term "mindness" is referring to the very core of samsaric mind, what it is at root, without all of its dualistic baggage. When this meaning is intended, it is quite wrong to translate it as "mind itself" as many have done, for that would lead to a major misunderstanding of what is actually being said.

Note that mindness is, in many cases, especially in the tantras, a path term. It refers to exactly the same thing as the term "actuality" or "actuality of mind" which is a ground term, but does so from the practitioner's perspective. It conveys the sense to a practitioner that he has baggage of dualistic mind that has not yet been purified but that there is a core to that mind that he can work with.

Muni: See under capable one.

Noble one, Skt. ārya, Tib. 'phags pa: In Buddhism, a noble one is a being who has become spiritually advanced to the point that he has passed beyond cyclic existence. According to the Buddha, the beings in cyclic existence were ordinary beings, spiritual commoners, and the beings who had passed beyond it were special, the nobility.

Prajna, Skt. prajñā, Tib. shes rab: A Sanskrit term for the type of mind that makes good and precise distinctions between this and that and hence which arrives at correct understanding. It has been translated as "wisdom" but that is not correct because it is, generally speaking, a mental event belonging to dualistic mind where "wisdom" is used to refer to the non-dualistic knower of a buddha. Moreover, the main feature of prajñā is its ability to distinguish correctly between one thing and another and hence to arrive at a correct understanding.

Realization, Tib. rtogs pa: Realization has a very specific meaning which is not always well understood. It refers to correct knowledge that has been gained in such a way that the knowledge does not abate. There are two important points here. Firstly, realization is not absolute. It refers to the removal of obscurations, one at a time. Each time that a practitioner removes an obscuration, he gains a realization because of it. Therefore, there are as many levels of realization as there are obscurations. Maitreya, in the *Ornament of Manifest Realizations*, shows how the removal of the various obscurations that go with each of the three realms of samsaric existence produces realization.

Secondly, realization is stable or, as the Tibetan wording says, "unchanging". As Guru Rinpoche pointed out, "Intellectual knowledge is like a patch, it drops away; experiences on the path are temporary, they evaporate like mist; realization is unchanging".

Reference and Referencing, Tib. dmigs pa: Referencing is the name for the process in which dualistic mind references an actual object by using a conceptual label instead of the actual object. Whatever is referenced is then called a reference. Note that these terms imply the presence of dualistic mind and their opposites, non-referencing and being without reference, imply the presence of non-dualistic wisdom.

Refuge, gzhi gnas: Skt. śharaṇaṃ, Tib. bskyab pa: The Sanskrit term means "shelter", "protection from harm". Everyone seeks a refuge from the unsatisfactoriness of life, even if it is a simple act like brushing the teeth to prevent the body from decaying un-necessarily. Buddhists, after having thought carefully about their situation and who could provide a refuge from it which would be thoroughly reliable, find that three things—buddha, dharma, and saṅgha—are the only things that could provide that kind of refuge. Therefore, Buddhists take refuge in those Three Jewels of Refuge as they are called. Taking refuge in the Three Jewels is clearly laid out as the one doorway to all Buddhist practice and realization.

Saṃsara, Skt. saṃsāra, Tib. 'khor ba: This is the most general name for the type of existence in which sentient beings live. It refers to the fact that they continue on from one existence to another, always within the enclosure of births that are produced by ignorance and experienced as unsatisfactory. The original Sanskrit means to be constantly going about, here and there. The Tibetan term literally means "cycling", because of which it is frequently translated into English with "cyclic existence" though that is not quite the meaning of the term.

Satva and sattva: According to the Tibetan tradition established at the time of the great translation work done at Samye under the watch of Padmasambhava not to mention one hundred and sixty-three of the greatest Buddhist scholars of Sanskrit-speaking India, there is a difference of meaning between the Sanskrit terms "satva" and "sattva", with satva meaning "an heroic kind of being" and "sattva" meaning simply "a being". According to the Tibetan tradition established under the advice of the Indian scholars mentioned above, satva is correct for the words Vajrasatva and bodhisatva, whereas sattva is correct for the words samayasattva, samādhisattva, and jñānasattva, and is also used alone to refer to any or all of these three sattvas.

Superior fact, Skt. paramārtha, Tib. don dam: This term is paired with the term "fictional" *q.v.* Until now these two terms have been translated as "relative" and "absolute" but those translations are nothing like the original terms. These terms are extremely important in the Buddhist teaching so it is very important that their translations be corrected but, more than that, if the actual meaning of these terms is not presented, the teaching connected with them cannot be understood.

The Sanskrit term literally means "a superior or holy kind of fact" and refers to the wisdom mind possessed by those who have developed themselves spiritually to the point of having transcended saṃsāra. That wisdom is *superior* to an ordinary, un-developed person's consciousness and the *facts* that appear on its surface are superior compared to the facts that appear on the ordinary person's consciousness. Therefore, it is superior fact or the holy fact, more literally. What this wisdom knows is true for the beings who have it, therefore what the wisdom sees is superior fact truth.

Superior fact truth, Skt. paramārthasatya, Tib. don dam bden pa: See under superior fact.

Superior fact truth enlightenment mind, Tib. don dam bden pa'i byang chub sems: This is one of a pair of terms; the other is Fictional Truth Enlightenment Mind *q.v.* for explanation.

Tirthika, Skt. tīrthika, Tib. mu stegs pa: This is a very kind name adopted by the Buddha for those who did not follow him but who, because they followed some other spiritual path, had at least started on the path to enlightenment. The Sanskrit name means "those who have arrived at the steps at the edge of the pool". A lengthy explanation is given in the *Illuminator Tibetan-English Dictionary* by Tony Duff and published by Padma Karpo Translation Committee.

Third order thousandfold world system, Tib. stong gsum 'jig rten:
Indian cosmology has for its smallest cosmic unit a single Mt.
Meru with four continents type of world system; an analogy
might be a single planetary system like our solar system. One
thousand of those makes a first order thousandfold world
system; an analogy might be a galaxy. One thousand of those
makes a second order thousandfold world system; an analogy
might be a region of space with many galaxies. One thousand
of those makes a third order thousandfold world system (1000
raised to the power 3); an analogy would be one whole universe like ours. The Buddha said that there were countless
numbers of third order thousandfold world systems, each of
which would be roughly equivalent to a universe like ours.

Tirthika, Skt. tīrthika, Tib. mu stegs pa: This is a very kind name
adopted by the Buddha for those who did not follow him but
who, because they followed some other spiritual path, had at
least arrived at the brink of the true path back to enlightenment. The Sanskrit name means "those who have arrived at
the steps at the edge of the pool" and comes to mean those on
the brink of actually crossing the river of samsara. A lengthy
explanation is given in the *Illuminator Tibetan-English Dictionary* by Tony Duff and published by Padma Karpo Translation Committee.

Unsatisfactoriness, Skt. duḥkha, Tib. sdug bngal: This term is
usually translated into English with "suffering" but there are
many problems with that. When the Buddha talked about the
nature of samsaric existence, he said that it was unsatisfactory.
He used the term "duḥkha", which includes actual suffering
but means much more than that. Duḥkha is one of a pair of
terms, the other being "sukha", which is usually translated as,
but does not only mean, bliss. The real meaning of duḥkha is
"everything on the side of bad"—not good, uncomfortable,
unpleasant, not nice, and so on. Thus, it means "unsatisfactory in every possible way". The real meaning of its opposite,

sukha, is "everything on the side of good"—not bad, comfortable, pleasant, nice, and so on. Therefore, that he is completely liberated from the sufferings actually means that he has completely liberated himself from the unsatisfactoriness of samsara, which includes all types of suffering and happiness, too.

Vajra Vehicle, Skt. vajrayāna, Tib. rdo rje'i theg pa: See under Great Vehicle.

Wisdom, Skt. jñāna, Tib. ye shes: This is a fruition term that refers to the kind of mind—the kind of knower—possessed by a buddha. Sentient beings do have this kind of knower but it is covered over by a very complex apparatus for knowing, that is, dualistic mind. If they practise the path to buddhahood, they will leave behind their obscuration and return to having this kind of knower.

The Sanskrit term has the sense of knowing in the most simple and immediate way. This sort of knowing is present at the core of every being's mind. Therefore, the Tibetans called it "the particular type of awareness which is there primordially". Because of the Tibetan wording it has often been called "primordial wisdom" in English translations, but that goes too far; it is just "wisdom" in the sense of the most fundamental knowing possible.

Wisdom does not operate in the same way as samsaric mind; it comes about in and of itself without depending on cause and effect. Therefore it is frequently referred to as "self-arising wisdom" *q.v.*

www.ingramcontent.com/pod-product-compliance
Lightning Source LLC
LaVergne TN
LVHW090409160726
843469LV00038B/575